ROCK 'N' ROLL WITH IT: OVERCOMING THE CHALLENGE OF CHANGE

Brant Menswar and Jim Trick

THE HYPE MACHINE:

"From the moment you open the book, Brant and Jim are amazing and insightful guides through the journey of change. Their knowledge, compassion, and willingness to share their stories and the story's others regarding the transformational power of change makes this a must read for teenagers to business leaders. A definite YES for those who want to keep teams or life moving forward!"

Sherry Dreger
Vice President of Marketing - Bentley Mills

"Often, change can lead to either evolution or revolution. Having the tools to navigate through both is critical to your success. Most of us aren't equipped for it, but this book gives you insight into how to turn change into opportunity. It provides a framework for you to use to assist in the constant challenge associated with change, and does it in a way that is unique, thoughtful and dynamic."

Bob Creviston
Chief Human Resource Officer - Universal Hospital Services

"It's one thing to talk about the weather. It's another thing altogether to sail a small boat through a hurricane and live to tell about it. Many authors write about change. Brant Menswar and Jim Trick both had excruciating, life-altering change thrust upon them. While they came out on the other side with bruises and scars, they were still breathing. With brutal honesty, they bare their souls and give you a map for making it through the frightening changes YOU face in your life. Rock 'N' Roll With It will change the way you look at change forever."

Marty Dodson
Songwriter (Kenny Chesney, Carrie Underwood, Blake Shelton)

"In Rock 'N Roll With It: Overcoming the Challenge of Change, Brant Menswar and Jim Trick provide an honest, relevant and inspirational guide to embracing and thriving with life's tidal changes... a must-read for anyone looking to foster a more productive relationship with the changes in their lives. We're all going somewhere, and Menswar and Trick help make the journey positive, fruitful, and fun. They've based their work on personal experiences and truths they have learned along the way, giving Rock N Roll With It a unique brand of candid friendliness that will lift your soul and remind you that change is a vital chapter in the book of happiness."

Frank (Skip) Yetter
Author (Rilertown)

"Brant and Jim don't just talk about change, they share change. Rock 'N' Roll With It offers authentic and rich stories from the authors as well as a mix of change masters, so readers can actually see multiple manifestations of change to help develop their own sea change when the moments arrive. Some of us may have found our voice and made a change and some of us are still warming up to our inspiration. Either way, Brant and Jim have provided plenty of anecdotes, laughs, exercises and tears to continue to stoke the change potential in each of us."

Mike Rozinsky
Director - Fidelity Investments

"Using the parallels of rock and roll as well as the guidelines of what it takes to achieve rock stardom, Trick and Menswar have created an honest and compelling book that's fun, funny, and informative. Trick and Menswar have lived it. They are the real deal. In this book, they share their most honest selves and provide the reader with the understanding that in order to be the rock star you want to be, you have to be committed, curious, and most of all, honest. These skills are the nuts and bolts of getting to a place of true freedom. Keep on rocking in this world. It's there if you want it."

Mary Lou Lord
Recording Artist

ROCK 'N' ROLL WITH IT:
Overcoming the Challenge of Change
Copyright © 2018 by Brant Menswar and Jim Trick. All rights reserved.
No part of this book may be used or reproduced in any manner whatso-
ever without written permission by publisher.

Published by:
Knight Speaker LLC
Winter Garden, FL 34787

Contact: Jim@KnightSpeaker.com

First Edition: January 2018

ISBN 987-0-9997296-0-1

Printed in the United States of America

Dedication

There are two kinds of lies

Some you tell, some you believe

You will rid yourself of both one day, and you will be relieved.

But you don't know now . . .

It's that story you're repeating

It's a picture in a frame

It's like a car crash, you can't look away,

and you may never be the same,

but I won't go there.

Because all's not lost, and you're not lost at all.

All's not lost, and you're not lost at all.

For the bruised and broken, the whole and healing,

and everyone in between.

ACKNOWLEDGMENTS

Writing this book was harder than we (a couple of road dog singer/ songwriters) could have ever imagined. It has taken the better part of two years and an incredible amount of support and patience from our friends and loved ones.

To our immediate families, the Menswar Family—Emily, Theo and Brady thank you for letting me disappear for hours each night to write this book, Mom and Dad, Todd and Karrie, Liz and Jim —and to the Trick Family: it's finally done! Thank you for loving us so selflessly.

Susan Shea, ED. S., BCBA, LABA, thanks for working diligently to make sure we look like we know what we're talking about.

Pam Kilgore, you won't have to listen to chapters being read to you like a Dr. Seuss book any longer. Thank you for your love and support.

To PW and JT, we offer a hearty "B'scuse me!" Love you, brothers.

NewSound, without you, there never would have been us. Alan Schaefer and the Banding People Together crew: thank you for teaching us to be rock star collaborators who literally wrote a book on a shared Google Doc—writing together, at the same time, on the same line. That is the power of True Collaboration^{SM}!

Jim Knight, your unbridled encouragement and support is what made us believe we could do this. Love you, bud.

To the beautiful, powerful, opinionated, blonde woman who stood up at a packed concert almost seven years ago to interrupt and challenge what you heard, your friendship and support amaze us. Thank you, Delilah!

Justin Spizman, your willingness to tell us when our writing was total crap is a major reason why we are proud of this project. Thank you for guiding us through this journey.

Rob Willington and the team at Swift Kurrent, your creativity and generosity were invaluable in bringing this to life.

To every venue, promoter, producer, and fan who has, for years, supported albums, concert tours, and this book, you have never let us down, and we are humbled by and grateful for you.

TABLE OF CONTENTS

FORWARD

To the Reader:

I have learned over the years that change is part of life. It is inescapable, constant, and, many times, overwhelming. But love it or hate it, it is absolutely present. The second you try and avoid it, it will remind you of its presence and challenge you in ways you never conceived possible. For me, the biggest challenge that comes with change is convincing my family and friends to get on board with whatever new path I am plunging down. I enjoy the challenge within change, and a life without change seems uneventful and dull.

Change doesn't just excite me. It totally energizes me, inspires me, and fuels my late-night jags of creativity on and off the air. I am thankful and appreciative for change. I often feel alone in my acceptance of change as many of those I love cringe at the very thought.

One recent change I experienced is that we moved my broadcasting studios from a building my staff and I had loved for over a decade. We chose a lovely turn-of-the-century craftsman home as our new place of business. But even after two years there, a few employees have refused to unbox their office decorations and family pictures, which still sit next to their editing stations. I believe they are thinking I might eventually buy back my original studio building so that they can move back in.

But the change is complete, and that ship has sailed. I want to help them adjust and cope with this unexpected change. So, perhaps, I will buy several copies of this wonderful book and subtly place it on the computer keyboards of my staff members and family members. I am sure that will help them to better accept and handle the pain of change.

As I contemplate adopting my fourteenth child, a baby boy with chronic health issues, I am bracing myself for the onslaught of naysayers who can't handle one more change in the dynamics of our family. They see it as a challenging and tremendous responsibility. While I understand their position, I also know this change will be for the better. We love growing our family, and giving the opportunity for a happy life to a young child is an absolute blessing. So, even though that change may come with plenty of opinions and feedback, it means the world to us.

I believe that the more we talk about change, the easier it will become to actually endure it. Change can be a welcomed addition to your life, if only you are prepared to face it head-on. With that said, thank you, Brant and Jim, for being transparent and kind in sharing your stories of change and, more important, your stories of redemption. You have given me a tool to share with many I love who have difficulty with changes. Perhaps, through your words and testimonies, they will learn not only to accept change but also to embrace it as a gift from the Lord.

—Delilah

INTRODUCTION
WELCOME TO THE JUNGLE

Dear Reader,

Rock 'n' Roll with It offers a unique approach to creating and accepting powerful change in your life.

For the last fifteen years, we have been fortunate enough to travel the world performing original music. Over the course of our careers, over a hundred-thousand people have been impacted by our work. From Central American refugee villages to main stages at popular music festivals, we have seen how music connects, inspires, and transforms.

We have always had the desire to use our music for more than just entertainment. In our lives, music has not only been our greatest influencer but also our most powerful tool to influence others. In fact, we have spent the last six years using music to teach True Collaboration℠ to everyone from NASA to Cisco to Microsoft through our work with Banding People Together, a consultancy of behaviorists, strategists, and real-life rock stars. We have helped these companies navigate change and create actionable plans to achieve their goals.

You might be wondering why a couple of musicians have chosen to pursue this work. The answer is multifaceted, but in the end it comes down to one word: redemption.

In school, Jim was always seen as "the fat kid." That unfortunate truth was coupled with a funny last name and a love for singing in the chorus, making him a perfect magnet for bullies. Food was always more than just food. It provided comfort, distraction, and, in some crazy way, friendship. In the summer of 1983, Jim's father became severely disabled. Jim's coping mechanism of choice? Overeating.

Morbidly obese and hopeless, he eventually underwent gastric bypass surgery. It worked for a while, but because Jim didn't understand the science of change, most of the weight came back. It wasn't until he did the real work essential to meaningful transformation that he was able to transform not only his body but also his entire life. Now 215 pounds lighter, Jim's passion is helping others cope with life's setbacks and conquer the change they long for.

Brant's personal story of change crescendoed when his healthy fourteen-year-old son, Theo, was suddenly diagnosed with a rare blood cancer. And 263 straight days in the hospital provided a chance to experience the kind of change that redefines what is truly important. After being told that Theo wouldn't survive the night, Brant had to sit on the edge of his child's bed to say goodbye and hear him say, "I'm going to miss you, Daddy."

Yet, the death sentence given to Theo got overturned when a daring act of creativity changed the "impossible" to possible. Thanks to a YouTube video appeal recorded by Brant's brother, Theo recovered and recently received his GED with honors, a year ahead of his class. He has enrolled in college to pursue a degree in video game design.

These stories of redemption prove that change, while incredibly challenging, is not impossible. Most of us have just never been taught how to approach and powerfully engage change in difficult situations. That is the reason you should read this book.

You have tried on your own and failed. You have started and given up. Now you're frustrated. We get it. Shit not only happens, but it has happened to you. Now you are sitting in it and telling yourself that change is "impossible." That's bullshit. How's that answer for rock-star swagger?

Rock 'n' Roll with It will provide you with an understanding of how change works and will equip you with specific strategies to accomplish the kind of transformational change that leads to the type of life you really want—one that bears fruit and enriches those around you.

We will use engaging interviews with change experts and clever metaphors from the music world to tap into the part of the brain that stores long-term emotional memory. We want you to be able to recall what you learn in this book as easily as you remember the lyrics to "Sweet Caroline." We will talk about change as though we are preparing for a concert. We will need to learn the songs, develop a set list, and then perform with passion and intention. Dare we say, you will become Rock Stars of Change!

Now, put on your leather pants and get ready to shake what your mama gave you.

CH-CH-CH-CH-CHANGES

THE UNIVERSALITY OF CHANGE

Norman Vincent Peale once said, "Change your thoughts and you can change your world." While, on the surface, this idea sounds like fortune-cookie advice, it's anything but a simple cliché found in a delicious cookie. The reality is that controlling your thoughts is complicated because not all thoughts are voluntary. When you factor in past traumatic events and emotional memories, our ability to control what we think is even more challenging. Emotions create thoughts, and thoughts create emotions. So, what happens when our thoughts are on the concept of change? For many, the mere mention of the word *change* stirs distinct emotions, some of which aren't entirely positive.

But the truth is, change is happening. Right now. We are in the midst of it. It's perpetual. It doesn't stop. Change is not to be feared, like that creepy uncle who comes around during the holidays or the loud bang that wakes you up in the middle of the night. Change is like breathing. The minute it stops, we are in trouble.

For as long as we can remember, change has been treated as risky and threatening. Like water cooler talk—those juicy, shocking tidbits of gossip—change-makers have kept us intrigued, wondering what they will do next. But it's time we stop perpetuating the lie that change is only for a few reckless, daring souls. We have it all backwards and need to relearn what change truly is and how it works.

Change, in and of itself, is not intrinsically hard or easy, good or bad. But, like it or not, it's inevitable. Everything exists in a perpetual state of change, movement, and evolution. Whether it is our bodies, relationships, or even our front lawns, one thing is for sure: nothing stays the same. Even things that seem inanimate are, at some mysterious, subatomic level, changing.

Most of the changes in the universe exist on a micro level and can't be seen or felt. Yet, when something as simple and present as our body temperature shifts, even only a few degrees, it can be a matter of life and death. You can't sense the constant cellular changes occurring right now within you, but when they morph or become cancerous, the power of that microscopic change, changes everything. Companies restructure, kids grow up, perceptions and desires contract and expand. The way your lover used to look at you is different now, and the dance steps required to maintain a relationship are practiced to the beat of an ever-changing rhythm.

Change is the norm. Change happens, whether you acknowledge it or not. You simply cannot control it. But how you respond and react to change is a choice all your own. Once you recognize that, you can harness the power of change and uncover the true rock star you have hidden within. Change should be an everyday conversation in which we identify the current obstacle, discuss the needed adjustments, and decide whether we need to "rock it" or "roll with it." Throughout this book, you will learn how to identify when to do each and how to go about it.

But before we get started, we'd like to explain why we are so passionate about change. Our stories are very different, but both reveal the full impact change can have on your life. Let us explain.

THE CHANGE WITHIN OUR LIVES

Deciding to make a change is an empowering, freeing decision that can put you on the path to a new and improved you. Digging deep and finding the courage to make the change is a difficult task—even for the most confident people. But, it is still your choice.

So, what happens when the choice is taken away? What happens when change is thrust upon you without your permission? Like the great Sam Cooke says, "A change is gonna come." That was the kind of change Brant experienced, and the following is his story in his own words.

As a self-proclaimed control freak of the highest order, it was hard to receive change I did not ask for. What my family and I experienced was difficult, at best, and seemingly impossible, at worst.

In May of 2012, my life was forever changed in the moment my eldest son, Theo, was diagnosed with a rare blood cancer called myelodysplastic syndrome. We were told that the only cure was a bone marrow transplant. He was fourteen years old. Any time I hear the word *cancer*, somewhere, in the depths of my mind, I can hear taps being played off in the distance at sunset. In my mind, death was not a question of "if" but "when." I know that isn't always the case, but when you hear your child has the "Big C," you immediately feel a lump in your throat that simply won't go away.

His younger brother, Brady, was immediately checked to see if he was a match. As is the case with 70 percent of all siblings, there was no match. So, the search began for someone to save my son. It only took a few months to find a "ten-point" match—perfect by all standards. It was a twenty-five-year-old male from the United States. That is the only information we were given, and we were happy to get that. All we cared about was the fact that Theo was going to be able to receive his transplant. Hallelujah!

We were told that the process would take thirty days in the hospital and seventy more days with several check-ups per week. Then, Theo would be back to living a normal life. The doctors were confident that the procedure would work and that Theo would recover quickly, as he was young and in good health.

In fact, Theo was in great health. He was a brilliant student. Ironically, we thought one day he would discover or create something that would change the world. A cure for cancer, perhaps? Now, I realize that every parent thinks his child is a genius, but Theo actually *is* a genius. He has an IQ score so high we didn't want to tell him in fear that he might think he could skate through life without really trying. He used words I needed to look up after a conversation, just to make sure I understood.

As every parent does, we had big dreams for our son. Now those dreams were in jeopardy. How could this happen? We didn't have a history of cancer in our family. Theo was a picture of perfect health—until he wasn't. Change hit us in the most awful of ways.

The countdown process for a bone marrow transplant begins on day "minus fourteen." That's when you begin your chemo regimen. Two weeks of that poison took its toll on Theo's young body, but he handled it like a champ and didn't get sick until the last few days. Then it was tough to watch. He couldn't keep anything down. He felt awful and just wanted to get cleaned up and rest. That's when it happened: "the shower."

Anyone who has ever had cancer knows exactly what I'm referring to. It's the shower you take when you have the sudden realization that your hair is falling out. One minute you are gently massaging shampoo into your scalp, and the next you are watching your hair fall to the drain in clumps. It's a stunning dose of reality about the gravity of the situation. Even though you know it's going to happen and you prepare yourself for the inevitable, it still comes as a shock—especially for a fourteen-year-old boy.

Theo received his transplant on August 12, 2012. We had prepared ourselves for some intense procedure, picturing a monster-sized needle stuck into his spine, slowly injecting marrow that would work its way into his bone. I guess we watch too many sci-fi movies because the transplant consisted of what looked like a bag of blood. They hung the bag above his bed and let gravity work the marrow into Theo's system. Big whoop.

We spent the next thirty days in the hospital while we waited for the transplant to take. Doctors call this process "engraftment," and when it finally happens the body starts to reproduce cells on its own. Staff ran blood tests every morning, and we would wait for the results to see if there was a spike in Theo's blood counts. While this is an exciting time of watching and waiting, it's a time of nervousness as well. When you suppress the body's immune system, bad things can happen. What if the transplant doesn't take? What if he contracts deadly bacteria or a virus?

Waiting for change. It sucks.

The process of change is very similar to the engraftment process. Often it takes an intense moment of vulnerability before the change actually happens. If we find the courage to actually make a change, then comes the dreaded waiting game. We wait for the change to "engraft." We look for signs that it's working.

While we waited for Theo's body to accept the new marrow, we were warned of something called graft-versus-host disease, or GVHD as doctors refer to it. GVHD is when the donated bone marrow doesn't recognize the body it is being transplanted into, and the donated marrow begins to attack the body. Once the new cells have reproduced enough, they recognize their new environment and stop the attack.

Everyone who receives a bone marrow transplant experiences GVHD in one of its four stages. Most people find themselves in stage one or two and recover quickly. If the disease progresses to stage four, it can be fatal. In that case, the cells are not recognizing anything and have started World War III in your body. The only treatment at this stage is to suppress the immune system to extreme measures. This, however, places the body at great risk for infection. This is where we found ourselves with Theo.

While they were suppressing his immune system, he contracted a deadly fungus called mucormycosis. The proper treatment for mucor is to boost the immune system so the body can attack the fungus. The two issues created a zero-sum game. The doctors pulled us into a room on March 23, 2013, and explained that no matter which issue they treated, the other would take his life. They suggested we say our good-byes as they thought he wouldn't make it through the night.

And then something miraculous happened: change.

My younger brother Todd, who lives fifteen-hundred miles away in New Hampshire, was devastated when he received the news. Unknown to my wife and me, he took five minutes and filmed a video of himself holding poster boards, explaining Theo's case, and pleading for help from anyone who could contribute. He uploaded the video to YouTube. Within forty-eight hours, the video had over five-hundred-thousand views. We received calls from people all over the world who believed they could help.

I received a call on my cell phone from Dr. Dimitrios Kontoyiannis at MD Anderson in Houston, Texas. He said, "I saw your video, and I believe I can help save your son." Dr. Kontoyiannis is one of the leading experts on mucormycosis, and his close friend Dr. Tom Walsh was the leading researcher on the fungus at Cornell University.

I then received a call from Dr. Tim Johnson, of *Good Morning America* fame. He told me to speak with our bone marrow doctor and tell him to make a list of any doctor he wanted to speak with in this country and he would make it happen within twenty-four hours. We did that, and Dr. Johnson connected us with Dr. Joseph Antin at Dana Farber Cancer Institute in Boston. Dr. Antin is the foremost expert on graft-versus-host disease. Together with our doctor, Dr. Yasser Khaled, the four physicians came up with a plan to treat Theo.

It worked. Theo recently celebrated his nineteenth birthday. While he continues to heal, we celebrate the power of change. It is the reason I approached Jim to write this book together. Theo's story provides us with all the proof we need to tell you that no matter what your circumstance, no matter what zero sum game you are facing, *change doesn't understand impossible.*

Jim's story presents a completely different perspective on change as his change wasn't forced upon him. Instead, he intentionally decided to make a positive change. Jim tells his story in the paragraphs that follow.

Like most eight-year-olds, I was excited that the hotel we were staying at had a pool. We had been to this particular hotel a year earlier, so I knew it was a particularly awesome pool. It was an indoor pool and part of the extended lobby. They had gone to great lengths to make it look and feel like it was outside. I'm sure the giant fake trees and plants that adorned the island in the middle of the pool did little to fool the grownups, but, to me, it was the height of exotic luxury.

My parents would sit in the hot tub while I ran back and forth. I loved the feeling of heating up in the Jacuzzi so that I could plunge myself into the comparatively freezing swimming pool water. The stinging rush of cold hurt in a way that felt dangerous, and in that moment, the notion that I could make choices that would affect my state became a conscious part of my human experience.

For whatever reason, the hotel didn't have many guests the previous year. It had felt like we owned the place. This year was more crowded, but not to the point where it dampened my enthusiasm. Bathing suits on, towels in hand, and excited to play in the pool, we made our way down. Friendly smiles welcomed us into the hot tub, and Mom warned me about the dangers of running too fast. She knew what was coming, and as I stepped into the hot tub, my plan was to thoroughly heat up so that the first leap into the pool would really count.

"I'm almost ready!" I warned.

My mom responded with, "Okay, but be careful. There's a lot of people here."

"Here I go!" I said, hoisting myself out of the caldron of bubbling, hot water.

"Alright, I'm watching," my mom replied.

I was hoping for a shock to my system, and I got one—just not the kind I was planning on. No, this was not from an icy dive into the hotel swimming pool. This shock came from the people in it. I reached the edge of the pool, and at the spot where I would have normally jumped in, there were two girls, a bit older than me, playing. Unlike the kind greeting I had gotten from the grown-ups in the hot tub, one of the girls looked at me and exclaimed, "You can't come in here! You are too fat!"

Fat jokes had started happening at school—not in full force and not to the extent they would eventually reach, but they had begun, and they hurt. Summer was a break from the bullies because they didn't live in my neighborhood. Being away at a hotel was a double layer of protection. My dad was in a good mood when we were away, and I always looked forward to his kinder version that emerged on vacation. Vacation was the safest place for me, or so I thought.

I wanted to cry, but I didn't. I walked back to the hot tub, crestfallen. My father was not a safe place to go, and I knew that awakening the rage-filled giant inside him wouldn't be good for anyone. Tears would have been seen as weakness and would have undoubtedly resulted in a spanking. The spanking would have been combined with an explosive, belittling speech, which I now realize was fueled by his own fear and self-loathing. It was him screaming at his own father and his own terrified little boy inside. Maybe he would have said something to the girls and maybe he would have confronted their dad. In any case, it would have ended with me worse for the wear.

The girls left the pool a little while later, and with them, they carried my joy. At the time, I didn't know that I had choice. At the time, I didn't know I could have taken my joy back. I got in the pool when they were gone, but it wasn't the same. I wasn't the same either. I had become the fat kid.

Middle school was hell, and the thing I chose for comfort was the very thing that was fueling my pain. Does this sound familiar?

Food continued to be my numbing agent, my escape, and seemingly my friend. As I got heavier, I also got funnier. Unlike many obese people who withdraw and hide, I developed a persona that was fun at parties and made people laugh and want to be my friend. The girls I liked only wanted to be my "friend," with a couple of exceptions. So I wore the double moniker of "fat kid" and "funny-friend guy." It was a lonely place, and the hidden pain almost never made its way to the surface. My size and personality were places I could hide.

The magnitude of this issue became clear years later on a sunny Saturday afternoon in 1991. My friends were off with their girlfriends or at work, and I was sitting alone in the parking lot of a Kentucky Fried Chicken. I was about to engage in my first hardcore binge. It was a family meal, with which I ordered three drinks, though I only wanted one. Ironically, it was a diet coke. Fat people love diet coke. I can't explain the diet coke addiction any more than I can explain how one person can eat eight pieces of fried chicken with sides of mashed potatoes and biscuits, but I did it.

No, I didn't feel sick, throw up, or feel any pain. I wish I had. I wish it hadn't tasted good, felt good, or provided comfort, but it did. It became normal, but as Bruce Cockburn once said, "The trouble with normal is it only gets worse."

Eight years later, a "normal" day of eating started with a breakfast of two bagels, one with extra butter and the other with extra cream cheese. Next, I stopped for an Egg McMuffin and two hash-brown patties. Once at the office, someone would say he was going to Dunkin Donuts and would ask if I wanted anything. Hell, yeah, I did: a sausage, egg, and cheese bagel and a vat of coffee. Lunch was what most people had for dinner, and before dinner, I'd have a Double Whopper as a snack. If dinner was with friends, it was usually grilled chicken on a salad, with a side of whatever lie I was telling about my metabolism or thyroid.

I remember one night I came home to find my electricity had been turned off. My financial life was as out of control as my eating. I had been out with friends and decided to end the day alone with a large pizza. There I sat, eating my pizza by flashlight before calling to have the power turned back on. I had become morbidly obese.

At 430 pounds, with a sixty-six-inch waist, I could not pee standing up, sit in a restaurant booth, buy clothes in a normal store, walk without my knees killing me, or fly in a plane without buying two seats. I was desperate, and you know what desperate times require.

My desperate measure was to lie down on an operating table at Massachusetts General Hospital. I had been warned about how dangerous gastric bypass was. Putting a morbidly obese person under anesthesia is very serious business. I wrote tear-soaked letters to my loved ones and left funeral instructions with a trusted friend. I went into surgery prepared not to come back.

In the months that followed weight loss surgery, the pounds melted off as if by magic. In the prep meetings, doctors would say things like, "Remember, this is a tool and not a cure." They warned us that the honeymoon period does not last forever and that this was a chance to get a head start and learn new habits. I pretended to believe them, but in my mind, I was thinking, "If people could really change, then we wouldn't need this surgery." I mean, I had a list of things I just knew would motivate me to change: health problems, sleep apnea, getting married. But one by one those things happened, and I didn't change. I convinced myself that this procedure was a magic bullet, even though the experts were adamant that it wasn't. Guess what? They were right.

I had a year or two as a thin man, and people were blown away. I was shopping for clothes at the places that had been off-limits. I could sit in chairs that, in the past, I would have broken. I could make love . . . Well, I will spare you the gory details of what it's like to have sex at 430 pounds. You're welcome.

I laid on an operating table, and surgeons cut off my stomach, re-routed my intestines, and, presto chang-o, I was cured. Or so I thought. I was starting to snack more. I reintroduced bread into my diet. I can actually remember the first dinner roll I ate two years after the operation. As my body healed from the procedure, it became easier to eat more, and I was ignoring the doctor's warnings and instructions. I had not been much for the gym, but any time I was putting in ceased. I started regaining the weight I had lost.

Some regain is considered normal and is actually expected. My problem was that it didn't stop. Eventually, I was back to the big and tall shop. I was back to worrying about whether chairs would hold me. Pound after pound and pant size after increasing pant size, I grew. The compliments on how great I looked stopped. The people around me knew what I knew but didn't want to think about: I was fat again.

I had tried and failed so many times that the thought of trying again was off the table. I had resigned myself to the thought that this was just who I was and how I was going to be. And, it wasn't just my weight that needed attention. I had a job that I was good at and paid well but drained my soul. My marriage was breaking down, and I had become generally dissatisfied with my life.

Henry David Thoreau writes, "The mass of men lead lives of quiet desperation. What is called resignation is confirmed desperation." The good news is that as my desperation grew, so did my curiosity. Curiosity is an amazing antidote for desperation and manifested itself in questions: "How did this happen?" and "What brought me to this place?" The more curious I became about my situation, the better the questions I asked. And as the questions improved, so did the answers.

One morning I woke up feeling inspired. I put on my sneakers and went on an early morning walk. As I made my way through the narrow streets of my beautiful little seaport town, my mind was racing and I decided to pray. I had all these questions and figured I'd seek divine wisdom. The question in my prayer was, "Why do we know what to do, but don't do it?" I got an answer. No, the clouds didn't part. There was no thunderous, audible voice, but I did get an answer, and then I got more questions. It became a perfect storm.

All these years later, the things that happened and the lessons I learned over the next month still blow my mind. The process of creating change in service of creating a rich, satisfying, impactful life is what compels me. Today, I am two hundred pounds lighter than I was at my heaviest, and I am working in accordance with my mission. Part of that mission is to serve you as you courageously and creatively identify and fulfill your mission.

In the end, we realize that change can be good, bad, both, or even neither. An incredible verse in the Foy Vance song "Two Shades of Hope" eloquently describes the two sides of hope. The hope that comes with change can hold both "enlightening" power in one hand and the darkness of a "hangman's rope" in the other.

Whether it's dealing with the change that occurs with an extraordinarily sick child or the everyday struggle with weight and overall health, we have all dealt with substantial internal and external change. It doesn't matter if it was forced upon us or we made a deliberate decision. Either way, change is there. It has pulled up a chair at the dinner table, and we need to acknowledge and engage with it. Ignoring it and pretending it doesn't exist will upset it, and it might even become an unruly, rude, unwelcomed guest that will wreak havoc on our families and us. We fear what we don't understand, and then tend to avoid what we fear. But change can't be avoided, so we must become more comfortable with change.

FEAR: UNCERTAINTY AND VULNERABILITY

So, why do we fear change? For starters, it can be overwhelming. But in reality even if it's not overwhelming, it does create a tremendous amount of uncertainty and vulnerability. As it relates to uncertainty, this brand of fear isn't born out of isolated circumstances, pessimism, or realism; rather, it's basic, human neurological programming. Neuroscientist Dean Burnett says, "In an evolutionary sense, the brain doesn't like uncertainty. Anything uncertain is potentially a threat."

Imagine you're on your way to an important work meeting. In one scenario, you get a flat tire and know for sure you'll miss the meeting; in the other, you're caught in stop-and-go traffic and don't know if you'll be late. Research suggests something surprising: we experience more stress when we don't know if something bad is about to happen than when we know for sure it's coming.

For example, neuroscientist Marc Lewis says, "Stop-and-go traffic is more stressful because, for survival reasons, the brain is evolved to pay a lot of attention to uncertainty. When consequences are unpredictable, dopamine floods a relatively primitive part of the brain called the 'action center,' activating a 'motor script that's ready to swing into action,' with your pupils dilating and your attention narrowing . . . You're going to expend the most energy when the outcome is least predictable and you have the greatest chance of influencing the odds."

However, uncertainty is truly appealing on occasion. Lewis indicates gamblers love the idea of "unpredictable good fortune." Either way, the unknown affects us all. "That's true with long-term uncertainty as well," Lewis says. "Anyone who's waited on the college admissions process can attest to how psychologically taxing such drawn-out scenarios can be. Long-term uncertainty is likely to lead to rumination, anxiety, cycling thoughts, and the development of expectations that will surely be biased by past experiences . . . We like to keep our future under (some semblance of) control.

"Our brains crave answers—now.

Ah, yes, control. Our brains are built to crave immediate information. Happiness researcher Dan Gilbert writes, "Human beings come into the world with a passion for control, they go out of the world the same way, and research suggests that if they lose their ability to control things at any point between their entrance and their exit, they become unhappy, helpless, hopeless, and depressed." We want to be able to imagine the future, and we want to be able to prepare for it. Uncertainty makes this awfully hard.

Journalist David McRaney, author of the bestselling book *You Are Not So Smart*, says the brain seems wired to resolve unknowns: "When the brain is facing uncertainty, it creates certainty; when it faces meaninglessness, it creates meaning." McRaney, who is now at work on a book about how people change their minds, also adds, "When you are uncertain, you have that immediate emotional reaction that it needs to be resolved now, and you will devolve to the fastest, easiest, least-painful solution before you will to the best solution."

Perhaps this could explain why, if you're considering applying for a dream job across the country, you might become overwhelmed by the unknowns: If I don't get it, will I be crushed? If I do get it, will I be good enough? Where would I live, anyway? At this point, you might decide to do the easiest thing of all and simply not apply. (It's probably not such a great job after all, right?) Of course, avoidance is a decision, too—a decision to maintain the status quo. You may do more and more research into what the job would be like, where you'd live, and who the other job applicants are. Trying to game the odds is useful up to a certain point, but it can eventually turn into a means of putting off change and welcoming in the appeal of doing nothing.

"One of the most de-motivating things for human beings is uncertainty, and we avoid it at all costs. In fact, we will just do nothing if we're not certain," says Margaret King, the director of a Philadelphia think tank called the Center for Cultural Studies & Analysis, which studies the role of culture and human behavior in consumer choice. "We're very, very hesitant to put resources at risk, and change is all about doing that."[1]

All of this to say, we are in fact pre-programmed to fear change. The cruel reality is that in a world of constant change, our very nature is to resist. Guess what? That is great news! That means it's not just *you*; it's all of us. We all have to deal with the natural resistance to uncertainty. So, let's say this together: *It is normal to fear change.*

The second side to the fear coin is an aversion to vulnerability. For

[1] https://www.unstuck.com/advice/afraid-change-science-uncertainty/

generations, we culturally saw vulnerability as a weakness. Due to the groundbreaking work of people like Dr. Brene Brown, we no longer see it that way. While uncertainty and vulnerability are bedfellows, neither needs to have a stranglehold on our ability to change.

Facing the unknown requires a high level of vulnerability in the form of considering and accepting all of the potential outcomes. While success and positive impact are achievable, loss, embarrassment, and pain are also very real possibilities. Even with a chance for success and positive impact, when the outcome is uncertain, we still view it as a threat. Our work as change-makers is to embrace our vulnerability as a strength while intentionally acknowledging and working against our intrinsic neurological programming.

Brene Brown defines vulnerability as "uncertainty, risk, and emotional exposure." Fear of uncertainty, risk, and emotional exposure is what keeps potential change-makers paralyzed. How often have you heard someone say he has a great idea or a change he wants to see in the world? However, when push comes to shove, most people demonstrate that they are in fact terrified to "put themselves out there," out where they can be seen by their family, friends, and community, in service of accomplishing this change.

As performers, we most commonly experience vulnerability as stage fright. For some of us, it's the butterflies of anticipation before we walk onto the stage. For others, it's a crippling, overwhelming fear of being exposed, a fear of not being as good as we think we are, or a fear of wearing our heart on our sleeve, only to be rejected or miss connecting with the audience at all.

Being vulnerable is hard. But if we are going to conquer and cope with change, the first two stops on the journey are fear and vulnerability. Because our natural tendency is to view uncertainty as a threat, we all experience a degree of something we like to call "change fright." Overcoming change fright includes acknowledging and bravely facing our fears, whether they be unsettling butterflies or crippling terror. While one cannot overcome a fear he is unwilling to face, the extent to which an individual does face his fear has a profound impact on his ability to overcome.

To prepare to overcome, you must be aware of two crucial points. In fact, we are going to list these as non-negotiables: commitment and forgiveness. If you cannot accept and live out these concepts, then you might as well put *Rock 'n' Roll with It* down and consider it the shortest book you've ever read. We hope you find what you are looking for, and if one day you are ready to take control of the change in your life, rather than allow change to control you, you can return to this page, and we can begin.

But before we outline the details of commitment and forgiveness, our non-negotiables, let's spend a little time with Andrea Kremer, who will help us see just what taking control of change in your life might look like.

ROCK STARS OF CHANGE: ANDREA KREMER

The *Los Angeles Times* has called two-time Emmy Award-winning sports journalist Andrea Kremer, "One of Television's best sports correspondents of all time." Kremer also teaches a class called the Art of the Interview at Boston University and regularly lectures at colleges and universities all over the country. If you think sitting down to interview one of the most respected sports journalists in American history is daunting, then you'd be correct. Kremer is known for asking tough questions in a way that people are compelled to answer. More engaged than intense, the first thing you notice about Andrea Kremer is that she is present. She never once looked at her phone or veered from the conversation at hand during our hour-long interview.

Andrea Kremer's career is an Original Song, written by someone who knows a lot about overcoming the challenge of change. "Wanna talk about change?" she asks. "Teenage girls come up to me and say, 'I want to be you.' But I didn't exist when I was their age." She goes on to say, "The only women that I saw were people like Phyllis George, and she was iconic, but she was appearing as Miss America on *NFL Today*. She didn't know about football. She was there because she was Phyllis George, former Miss America. There were no female sportscasters. They weren't reporting or delivering sports news. So, it's not like I was there saying, 'I'm gonna break that glass ceiling.' I mean, that's just not the way it was." Creating intentional change for Kremer was about becoming something that had never existed before.

While there may not have been a pool of hard-hitting, female sports journalists to inspire Kremer when she was a kid, there was always football. Kremer says the following about her love of the game: "Every year since I was about ten or eleven, the week before the Super Bowl, I would collect the articles from the *Philadelphia Enquirer* and the now defunct *Philadelphia Bulletin* and *The New York Times*. I would cut them out, paste them on a piece of paper, and on Super Bowl Sunday morning, I would present my parents with a scouting report for the game. I was either doomed to be a PR person or become a journalist."

While other parents might have encouraged their daughter to pursue more typical pastimes, Andrea's parents were different. Kremer continues, "I loved sports. I happened to know more than most of the boys, and my parents thought it was great. They bought me books, and my dad got us season tickets to the Philadelphia Eagles. We went every week. Our Sundays revolved around football. We either went to the games, or we sat and watched the games. We got cheesesteaks, and all the brilliant accouterments, then sat and watched, every single week."

While Kremer credits herself with teaching her parents about football, she says, "Encouragement from my parents, from a very young age, was the most seminal event that helped launch my career." Her takeaway was that she was fortunate to have people in her life who understood her passion and encouraged it. Passion and encouragement on their own are nice, but combining the two offers limitless potential.

It needs to be said that while Andrea Kremer is, indeed, passionate about football, she is also passionate about storytelling. She says, "Everyone has a story to tell, and being able to dig deep and find that story is fascinating to me. One of my strengths is connecting with people, getting them relaxed, and getting them to talk."

Kremer's first job was working as the sports editor for Pennsylvania's largest weekly newspaper. At that time, she worked on a story about the economic impact on a city hosting the Super Bowl.

Philadelphia was trying to become a host. And for the first time, NFL Films was going to do a promotional video for the state. Kremer found it interesting and set up an interview with one of the top people at NFL Films.

She was offered a tour after the interview. She had to try to play it cool. "I had loved football since I was eight years old, and I had reached nirvana," Kremer recalls. "I looked at my watch and said, 'Yeah, I guess I have some time.' Inside, my heart was beating, and then he walked me to my car and said, 'It's interesting; you're the kind of person we really try to hire, someone who knows how to write and really knows football.' That night, I went home and told my mom about the conversation, and she said, 'Apply right now!'"

It was 1984, and Kremer had to stay put because they were heading into the Los Angeles Olympics. Able to get any interview she wanted, Kremer worked so hard on that event that she developed mono and wound up watching the Olympics from her couch. As the Olympics came to a close, she remained at a crossroads. She had transformed her newspaper's sports section, but was ready for change. She describes it as "a great first job, but I was done."

Andrea tells this story: "I went to NFL Films, and they made me take a test to confirm my football knowledge. They said, 'We're gonna let you know in a week.' I applied in September. The timing was perfect. They had just started producing rock videos, so they had a dearth of producers and needed them. One week later, I got the job."

Kremer became the first female producer/editor ever hired by NFL Films. At that moment in the interview, Andrea Kremer looked me square in the eye and smiled: "That's change for ya."

Kremer would eventually go on to work for CBS Sports, ESPN, NBC, HBO, and *NFL Magazine*. She has worked in every facet of sports journalism for decades. From sideline reporting Super Bowls and Sunday Night Football to her current work on HBO's *Real Sports with Bryant Gumbel*, Kremer's drive and commitment has resulted in meaningful work that has been appreciated by sports fans and acknowledged by her industry.

She sees her accolades and awards as an indication that she has been around for a long time, that her work has been consistent, and while she notes that it's nice to be recognized by people, she, in a strong tone, says, "If you set out to do your job for that reason, then you're screwed. You shouldn't do your job thinking you're going to get accolades or awards." Motive is important to Kremer, and she believes that seeking that kind of approval is, as she puts it, a "misguided priority." "In my business," Kremer states, "you're only as good as your last story. The minute you start resting on your laurels, I think you're done."

She shares this memory as I ask what drives her to excel: "I used to dance ballet. I was in a high-level class and watching another group. I was in the back, looking at the girl in the front. Her leg was up by her ear, and she could do four pirouettes. My leg could only get to my shoulder, and I could only do three pirouettes. I remember thinking, 'If she can do that, why can't I do that?' And all of sudden, I literally thought to myself, 'What is that thought doing for me? How is that helping me? Don't worry about her. You can't do anything about her. You can only do something about yourself. Focus on yourself if you want to get your leg higher or do another rotation.'" She continues by adding, "I'm a very competitive person. Of course I want the best stories, but that's because I want to be able to do my best." She then summarizes her drive and competitive nature with the following statement: "I compete against myself."

While Kremer is indeed a driven and committed individual, she is not an island; she happily submits herself to honest critique: "I *love* feedback. I *crave* feedback. If you just tell me, 'Good job,' it's almost like an insult. I don't need to be stroked. Tell me what was good, but tell me what could have been better." According to Kremer, not all feedback is helpful. She says, "A lot of people just say stuff because they want to be contrary, but I welcome feedback from people I respect."

This led to a conversation about self-talk. Kremer says she struggles with a fair amount of negative self-talk: "Bad Andrea beats up on

Good Andrea." She continues by saying, "Many people have a loop that runs in their head that's negative. You have to fight that. You hear it. You acknowledge it. You pay it its due, and then tell it, 'You're not helping me. You're not benefiting me in any way, so go away.'" Kremer acknowledges "Bad Andrea" so that she can weigh what that voice is saying: "If it does offer something true, thank it, and then send it away."

In 2001, Kremer was named one of the most influential mothers in the United States. But the road to becoming a mom was anything but easy. She tells the story: "I was your stereotypical career woman. I was totally focused on my career. On a personal level, I was never one who said, 'Oh, my God, I've got to have children,' or, 'Oh, my God, that's the cutest baby. I wanna hold it.' I never begrudged anybody, but it just wasn't me."

She and her husband talked about it and decided it was important. So, they decided to try. At this point, she comically says, with an ooh-la-la inflection, "Oh, yeah . . . we'll try." She goes on to say, "As it turns out, I hit thirty-eight, thirty-nine, and all of a sudden, it felt like a sort of explosion of, 'Oh, my God, I won these Emmys, I've broken these stories, I've covered all these events . . . What do I have to show for it? What's my life? Where's my life gonna be when I'm older? Is this what my life is about—just these work accomplishments?'" The decision to have a baby was set, though she went into the process with her eyes wide open.

She explains, "When you're a Type A—or, as I've been described, a Type-A-squared personality—and you're in your late thirties and you want to try to have a baby, it's not for the faint of heart." Kremer would endure multiple miscarriages before finally giving birth to a beautiful baby boy. She says, "I'm very lucky that I did have a child, and it's by far the greatest experience of my life. I can't even imagine what it would have been like not to have a child."

Kremer talks about others' reaction to her decision to become a mom at the height of her career. She recounts some of those interactions: "People would ask, 'How are you going to be able to work, and how are you going to be able to travel? Your life's gonna change.' And I'd look at them and (sarcastically) say, 'You're right. I'm going to be the first working mother who travels in the history of the world.'" Andrea Kremer has been described as someone who "came out of the womb determined." And she goes on to say, "I firmly believe that you can do anything that you set your mind to."

As you can tell from Andrea's approach to life and work, she clearly believes what's worth being done is worth doing well. This is exemplified in her decision to nurse. She shares the following story: "I was about eight months pregnant, and my husband says, 'Ya know, I'd really like you to nurse for close to a year,' and I was like, 'Sha . . . you'll be lucky if you get six months out of me.' Twenty-two months later, the only reason that I stopped nursing was that I got pregnant again. We shipped breast milk all around the country on dry ice, and we made it happen. I'm kind of the template for other young women who do that today. That was a commitment that we made to our child."

As we have stated, commitment is key when it comes to creating and dealing with change. Kremer talks about the lengths she went to, determined to keep the commitment she made to breast-feeding: "I've pumped breast milk in most of the red-carpet clubs and sports arenas in America." She tells a story about her cooler full of breast milk sitting outside the office of a team's head coach. An intern asked Kremer what was in there. Before she could answer, the coach burst from his office and said, "That's personal! You don't ask her those questions!" She talks about how protective he was of her and what it was like to be pregnant or nursing during a whole NFL season. The players and coaches looked out for her. She also repeatedly makes the point that she wouldn't have been able to do any of it without the love, support, and encouragement of her husband, noted archeologist John Steinberg. His support would continue to be essential as the challenging next chapter of their lives unfolded.

Kremer had said she stopped nursing because she became pregnant again, but she further explains: "We lost that baby at four and half months, which, aside from losing my mother, was the most traumatic event of my life."

She shares, "When I lost the baby, it was during the playoffs, and I still looked pregnant for several weeks. I was at the Super Bowl, and people were asking, 'When are you due?' It was brutal. It was so brutal . . . I can't even tell you. You're not pregnant but you look pregnant, and everyone's asking you about it. What do you say? What do you say?"

She then remembers the people who came along side of her: "There was a coach that I was pretty close with his wife. One day they came by our ESPN studios, and I pulled her aside, and I told her. She looked at me and said she had lost a baby for the exact same reason. The same chromosomal thing . . . the same exact one. I looked at her, and she hugged me. She understood. Just by virtue of that, she made me feel better. Having her there was a great comfort, and yet again, the single most important person in all of it was my husband. I felt like I let him down, but never for one single second would he accept that or want me to feel that way."

The process of overcoming the challenge of this unintentional change required this strong, determined, powerful journalist to find comfort in the arms of those who had walked through the same fire. It was in allowing herself to be vulnerable that she was able to heal. Kremer recalls a dear friend who had been through a similar situation and called her. "I just started crying. She talked me off the ledge. In that moment, I needed to know that I wasn't alone. I wasn't the only person who has experienced this. This is okay. This is normal, and it's okay to feel this way. It's gonna pass. Other women have felt this way, and it's not just you." She goes on to say, "There's always this feeling of, 'No one understands me. No one's ever felt this way.' When a peer/friend tells you that she has felt this way, it's a big exhale."

It's clear during this part of the interview that she is not only sharing for the sake of a book on change but also for the people who, like her, would find comfort in knowing that they are not alone. When we ask what she would say to a woman in a similar situation, she replies, "From a medical standpoint, you go through all the things that happen physically, but what they don't tell you is that you go through all the postpartum stuff—except there's no baby . . . There's no reward, and that's really hard. They don't prepare you for that. It just hits you. So, you have to be prepared for that."

We talked about dealing with grief, not only as it relates to losing her baby but to losing her mother as well. Kremer, who lost her mother over twenty years ago, says she still misses her daily. "Grief," Kremer says, "is so personal. I wouldn't offer advice, but there is a perspective, and I think it's an important perspective. I got the diagnoses from my mother. When she told me about it, face to face, all I could think was, 'Oh, my God, how am I going to deal with this? How am I going to live without her? Who am I going to call? She's never going to see me get married. She's never going to meet my child.' It didn't occur to me until I had a child what she was going through. What she was thinking." Kremer sees the shifting from her own lens to how her mother must have been feeling as helpful and says, "She was thinking, 'I will never see my daughter get married. I will never meet my grandchild. I won't see where my daughter is going to go in her career.' So, I offer that as a perspective."

One of the things Andrea Kremer has learned from enduring loss is not to put things off: "When you suffer a loss, the cliché people say is you have to live every day to its fullest. Do we really do that? No, we don't. But, here's what I do. I don't say, 'I'll do it next year.' This is the change that came from the death of my parents. I don't know what's going to happen next year. If I can do it now, I do it now. Waiting does nothing for you. It doesn't mean be reckless, but what good comes from waiting?"

The lessons to be gleaned from Andrea Kremer's life and career cover the vast spectrum of what it means to truly overcome the challenges of change. Nothing was off limits during our time with Kremer. She never told us to turn off the recorder so that she could tell us the "real" story. Andrea Kremer possesses a confidence, consistency, and transparency that supports her role as world-class game-changer. And now that we've shown you how Andrea embraced change over the years, that leaves us with one question for you: are you ready for change?

OUR NON-NEGOTIABLES FOR CHANGE

Lasting change is nearly impossible to achieve without two things:

1. Commitment

2. Forgiveness

Remember how we said uncertainty and vulnerability work together to drive fear? The solution to overcoming that fear also requires two things to work together: commitment and forgiveness. We need a level of commitment from you that warrants the change you seek.

But, here is the challenge. Many of us rarely commit 100 percent to anything. We can come close and may even reach 100 percent for a brief moment, but life and circumstances wear us down, and our commitment level wanes. When we experience struggle, it threatens our ability to achieve the change we seek. Many times, when trouble comes, we hit pause on our change journey and temporarily halt our process. Days can become weeks, weeks become months, and yada, yada, yada . . . paralysis.

How do we get unstuck? How do we stop from just saying, "F*** it?" We find our answer in another "F" word: forgiveness. Let's start with self-forgiveness, the most important kind of forgiveness for the purposes of our conversation.

When we are 100 percent committed to something, when we give it everything we have and we fail, we can be quick to forgive ourselves because we know we tried our best. We can look back at our effort and find solace in the blood, sweat, and tears it took to get there. However, if we didn't give it our full commitment, if we phoned it in and half-assed it, then our ability to forgive ourselves for the failure diminishes. We punish ourselves, thinking we didn't really "buy in" or try as hard as we could have. At best, this behavior brings whatever progress we were making to a complete stop; at worst, it serves as a white flag of surrender.

This is really important: *we don't expect 100 percent commitment from you.* What we do expect is a strong commitment to either achieve the change you seek or handle the change thrust upon you. And, most important, *we expect you to forgive yourself when you fail.*

We don't want to ruin the end of this story for you, but spoiler alert: you are going to fail. Some time and in some way, we all do. That's okay. What we need to do is forgive ourselves for not giving 100 percent effort and then get back on the stage to sing another song.

We would be remiss not to also mention the power of forgiving others. As Jonathan Lockwood Huie puts it, "Forgive others, not because they deserve forgiveness, but because you deserve peace." While forgiving ourselves is crucial on our journey toward change, forgiving others has a profound effect on our ability to stay motivated. With peace comes prosperity. If we truly want to achieve the change we seek, forgiving those who have wronged us clears the path to keeping our commitments.

How strong does your commitment need to be? It's different for everyone. The commitment needs to be strong enough to weather the waiting. Lasting change doesn't happen overnight. It's a process. Brant experienced this in the search for a diagnosis and cure for his son's cancer. The initial lab results were inconclusive, due to the cells in Theo's body literally being in the process of change. It wasn't until the change was complete that the doctors could accurately diagnose the problem. It took six months to reach that point. After Jim had gastric bypass surgery, he still needed to wait for this new change to produce the results he was looking for. It took months of waiting and working before Jim saw the benefit of his change.

Tom Petty says it best when we hear him sing, "The waiting is the hardest part." *But the waiting is part of the changing.*

Some of us have the willpower to follow instructions to a "T" and never veer off course, no matter what life throws at us. Others will need a cheat day to stay energized amidst the stresses of daily life. No matter where you fall on that scale, you must be able to accept the bad days, forgive the failures and mistakes, refocus on the next performance, and stand firm while you wait for the results you are looking for. If you can do that, you can shift the paradigm.

COMFORT FOR YOU

30% OFF*

NOW THROUGH APRIL 8TH
SHOP IN-STORE AND ONLINE

Clarks

IN STORE CODE:

ONLINE COUPON CODE: BGP-SXYT-APLS-WXYT

SRDM1815Q028S0053FV

Clarks

60 TOWER ROAD
WALTHAM, MA 02451

Postmaster please deliver 3/19, 3/20, 3/21

Visit a Clarks store near you or shop online at www.clarksusa.com:
Crossgates Mall Albany

75827-US-F*********************AUTO**ALL FOR AADC 120   T26   P1   23257
Cathy Jordan
21 Coventry Dr
Clifton Park NY 12065-1747

COMFORT IN YOUR SOUL

#CLARKSFORLIFE

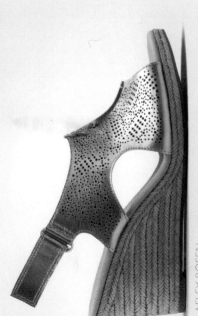

LAFLEY ROSEN

SHIFTING THE PARADIGM

Realizing and accepting that change, on all levels, is inevitable not only has the potential to alleviate fear, but it also invites us to find our place in the natural expansion of the universe. Father Richard Rohr says, "Change asks us to let go, and we're not good at letting go. We're good at holding on."

We've been programmed to believe in the age-old adage, "A bird in the hand is worth two in the bush." We have accepted that proverb as truth because of the perceived threat of uncertainty, but we need to let that bird go and start with empty hands. We need to forget about what we think we know about change and be willing to write a new song. Or, at the very least, we must learn a new way to play an old song. So, how are we going to do that?

Let's look to the great philosopher Robert Plant who tells us not to be alarmed if there is a bustle in your hedgerow because it's just a spring clean for the May Queen. The classic lyrics from rock 'n' roll's greatest anthem, *Stairway to Heaven*, allude to the busy, ritualistic cleaning during springtime. This includes deciding what we keep and what we will discard as we begin washing the windows and cleaning the baseboards to prepare for the "May Queen," a maiden chosen by a town to characterize the hopes and potential for the coming year. She is a symbol of beauty, spring, and new beginnings.

As we begin our journey into conquering change, we will need to do some spring cleaning and decide what we will keep (what we find certain) and what we will recycle or throw away.

Over the next few chapters, we are going to separate what you truly value from what you are feeling at the moment. We will help you find your "non-negotiables." We are going to determine the type of change you are facing and, depending on your commitment level, explore several strategies to achieve the change you seek. Over that process, you will discover your authentic voice, learn how to use it to drive positive change, create a plan to follow, and learn how to deal with the critics who stand in your way of becoming a Rock Star of Change.

We aren't looking for one-hit wonders who play their smash hit and walk off the stage. We are looking for legendary artists who have the will to grind it out and the fortitude to play through broken strings, forgotten lyrics, and an unappreciative audience. This journey will have massive highs and unforgettable lows. But if you can endure, if you can conquer your fear and accept your forgiveness, what you thought was possible for your life will change. It will grow. The impact you will make in this world will increase. The legacy you leave behind will be worth remembering. If that's not the stuff of rock 'n' roll legend . . . then what is?

HEY, NOW, YOU'RE A ROCK STAR

ROCK 'N' ROLL WAS BIRTHED OUT OF CHANGE

In the late 1940s and early 50s, a new style of music caused quite a scene. As most of America was quietly enjoying the musings of legendary crooners like Frank Sinatra and Perry Como, a swell was forming among the younger generation. A raucous style of music that made references to everything from sex to illicit behavior was not only becoming popular but was also engaging youth in literal call and response fashion. In a time of extreme conservatism and segregation, the merging of black culture and white suburban youth—who were swinging their hips to these infectious rhythms—went over like a Led Zeppelin (a similar clash of opposites produced the legendary group's name).

Rock 'n' roll was birthed from change. The merging of black and white culture may account for arguably the largest amount of change in the history of our country. But, it wasn't just the physical change of unifying public places that all races could use; it was also a change in thought as to what was right and wrong. It was a change in perspective and understanding, a new awareness of how 245 years of slavery affected our country. Rock 'n' roll was at the forefront of all that change.

Long used as a euphemism for sex in African-American culture, *rock 'n' roll* became the term used to describe the clash of "hillbilly music" with rhythm and blues. Famous disc jockey Alan Freed is credited with first using the term to describe the music he played on his radio show. That music is best exemplified by none other than the "King" himself, Elvis Presley.

Elvis was the embodiment of rock 'n' roll. A great-looking, young white man, who sounded like a black man, he steeped his music and movements in sexuality. This music forged change. Describing lips like "volcanoes," swinging his hips to the delight of young women everywhere, and curling that upper lip to entice anyone watching may seem tame in this day and age, but it was downright smutty back then. Rock 'n' roll music pushed the boundaries of freedom and accepted practices in 50s culture. Elvis not only changed the face of popular music, he changed pop culture.

In the mid-50s, there were scarce recordings from African-American artists. Their earning potential in relation to their impact on popular music was way out of balance. That is, until Elvis unlocked the potential to tip the scales. You see, Presley purchased the catalog of an African-American songwriter named Otis Blackwell. Blackwell was one of the earliest influences on rock 'n' roll. How influential you ask? His songs include "Fever," "Great Balls of Fire," "Don't Be Cruel," "All Shook Up," and "Return to Sender." Elvis watched as his own company, Gladys Music, hired a gifted black songwriter named Claude Demetrius, who went on to write "Hard Headed Woman," the first rock 'n' roll single to earn an RIAA Gold Record.

Looking back, it shouldn't have been as surprising as it was. It is completely normal for something birthed from change (rock 'n' roll) to actually become the impetus for even more change. As the decades have passed, rock 'n' roll has continued to morph and create new genres of music, like punk, metal, and hip-hop. Even modern EDM music finds its roots in rock 'n' roll.

Rock 'n' roll continues to change because it *is* change. It is a reflection of our constantly changing culture. To stay relevant and influential, it has to embrace change and stay on the forefront of modernity. It shines a mirror back on all of us, letting us take a good look at ourselves to see if we like the reflection we are faced with.

Even Michael Jackson, the King of Pop, reflects in his famous words in "Man in the Mirror" that changing the world starts with us. The point of this walk through rock 'n' roll history? If we are going to change our world, it starts with us.

DEFINING A "ROCK STAR": ROCK STARS CAN EXIST OUTSIDE OF MUSIC

When it comes to change, each of us is the lead singer in his own rock band. We can all become confident, charismatic, well-practiced, and completely in control. You know it when a real rock star enters the room. The energy changes and so does the focus. The air feels almost electric, raising the hairs on the back of your neck. Girlfriends swoon—hell, even the boyfriends swoon—while the rock star remains seemingly unfazed.

Jim recalls his experience with a larger-than-life rock star: "In the fall of 2002, I touched Bono. I'm sure he has no memory of it, but I talked about it for months after it happened. I was front row for the Elevation Tour, and he reached down to hold my friend's hand. Those around us reached up and held on to his sweat-covered wrist. When he moved on to the next fan, we felt like Jesus had come to town. Again, sometimes even the boyfriend swoons."

If you are like us, you'd expect to see a picture of Bono when you look up *rock star* in the dictionary. He is the quintessential example. He wears his sunglasses not only at night but *inside* as well. His fans include heads of state, African orphans, three generations of people all over the world, and even the Pope. It has been said that it is more difficult to get an appointment with Bono than the President of the United States.

Bono's sphere of influence goes far beyond music. Through his work with (RED), the ONE Campaign, Amnesty International, the Clinton Global Initiative, EDUN, Make Poverty History, MusiCares, and UNICEF, just to name a few, he uses his rock-star status to drive the change he wants to see in this world.

However, being a rock star is more than just using your influence to drive change. Consider the example of Rick Allen, another literal rock star, whose band has sold over one-hundred-million records and has toured for over forty years. Rick Allen is not a household name, but you know his band and his story. His band is Def Leppard, and Rick Allen is the drummer who, at the height of fame, lost his arm in a horrific car accident. Shortly after, he said, "You know, people have said to me, 'I don't know what I would have done if I'd have gone through what you went through.' I just turn around and say, 'Well neither did I.' Until you discover that part of yourself, it's inexplicable. You just have to go through the experience, and somehow you're inspired."

Losing his arm didn't stop him. Powerful determination, mixed with evolving technological innovation, has allowed Allen not only to continue drumming but also to serve as an inspiration to others who have been rocked by unexpected change. His Raven Drum Foundation serves, educates, and empowers veterans and people in crisis. Allen's work with Camp Kilpatrick has impacted the lives of young people sentenced to juvenile detention facilities. When he isn't recording and touring, he and his wife travel the world leading workshops and developing products to make a difference in the lives of people suffering from disabilities. Rick's mascot is a caricature called Stick Rick, whose motto is simply, "Life is great! Be a rock star!"

While Bono and Rick Allen are "textbook" rock stars for all the reasons you would think, truth be told, being a real rock star has little to do with music. The kind of real rock stars we are talking about are not motivated by groupies and fame. Real rock stars have four things in common:

1. They drive change and take risks.
2. They develop their own voice.
3. They are on the front lines of creating something new.
4. They have enough swagger to carry them through difficult times.

If we are going to become Rock Stars of Change, we have to develop each of these characteristics. Once we do, we are able to take difficult situations and respond to them in a powerful way. Only from this place of strength can we create meaningful, effective solutions.

CENTER STAGE

As we look at the characteristics of a rock star, please understand that your individual motivation will have a significant impact on your ability to achieve and maintain rock-star status. We will address motivation later in the book, but for now, let's dive deeper into the essential attributes of real-life rock stars.

1. Rock Stars Drive Change and Take Risks

At the end of the day, rock stars are driven to achieve meaningful impact—for both crowds and individuals. Do you remember the story of the little boy who frantically tries to rescue hundreds of dying starfish washed up on the beach? A man walks by and discourages him, "With so many stranded, you will never be able to make much of a difference." The boy bends down, picks up yet another starfish, and throws it as far as he can back into the ocean. He then turns, smiles, and says to the man, "I made a difference to that one!"

A Rock Star of Change is driven to make a difference by changing what is possible for someone (including himself) or for everyone. When it comes to measuring impact, consider the words of another rock star, Gandhi:

> It's the action, not the fruit of the action, that's important. You have to do the right thing. It may not be in your power, may not be in your time, that there'll be any fruit. But that doesn't mean you stop doing the right thing. You may never know what results come from your action. But if you do nothing, there will be no result.

Certainly, costs must be considered when facing significant obstacles. A real rock star weighs the risks against the potential results. But even then, the choice of doing nothing is never a consideration. Nothing produces . . . well, nothing. The risks are never a deterrent. They are merely another challenge to achieving the end result.

In the end, rock stars take risks that push the envelope to really uncomfortable and, at times, seemingly dangerous places. But they do it without going so far as to be unable to come back to a safer place. For many of us, we have drawn a way-too-safe line, far from the edge.

Author and speaker Rob Bell is someone who intentionally lives close to the edge. A headache put an end to Rob Bell's dream of textbook rock stardom. His band Ton Bundle had been playing shows in Chicago and was starting to get some attention. With weeks' worth of high-profile club dates booked, you can imagine how Rob felt when his headache turned out to be viral meningitis. If a doctor telling you the fluid around your brain has become infected and is essentially squeezing your brain into your skull isn't a good reason to cancel a tour, we don't know what is. Up to this point, the band was his life. When he was finally well enough to get back to playing, his band had lost both momentum and enthusiasm. Ton Bundle broke up, leaving Rob to answer the question, "Now what?"

Friends answered his question by suggesting he become a pastor, which at first seemed ridiculous. But the more he sat with this nutty idea, the more it actually made sense. While teaching water skiing at a summer camp, he offered to give a talk because the camp pastor wasn't available. Presto! This ridiculous suggestion became his calling.

Shortly after seminary and a season of working in a traditional church, he and his wife, Kristen, decided to take a huge risk and try something different. With no clever billboards or outreach campaigns, they, via word-of-mouth, held a "gathering" in a school gymnasium. One-thousand people showed up. Within a year, Rob, Kristen, and their team had an entire defunct shopping mall donated to them. They called their new community Mars Hill, and within a couple of years, over ten-thousand people were meeting weekly there. In his spare time, Rob started producing an acclaimed video series called *NOOMA* and writing books that would go on to become *New York Times* bestsellers.

In 2011, Rob took another huge risk with *Love Wins: A Book about Heaven, Hell, and the Fate of Every Person Who Ever Lived. Love Wins* asks questions about the core of Christianity that rocked his evangelical following. The criticism and shunning that came from a number of fundamentalist denominations and organizations did not deter Rob from continuing his mission. In 2011, *Time* named Bell one of the hundred most influential people in the world. He left Mars Hill in 2012 to create a global platform from which he could teach, preach, and redefine the sermon as an art form.

In 2013, his follow-up book, *What We Talk about When We Talk about God*, made it to Oprah's Book of the Month Club. The next year, he traveled with Oprah, Deepak Chopra, and Elizabeth Gilbert for Oprah's Live Your Best Life Tour. During his 2016 How To Be Here tour, Rob shared multiple stories of his projects that failed on one or more levels. An innate desire to drive change leaves Rob Bell undeterred. As it relates to success or failure, one of the key pieces of advice

Rob routinely offers is that all creative work is a risk, and our job is simply to "do the work and surrender the outcome." Rock stars do the work needed to experience the change they seek.

2. Rock Stars Develop Their Own Original Voice (OOV)

In the 2001 cult-classic film *Rock Star*, Mark Wahlberg plays Chris "Izzy" Cole. Cole is the lead singer in a Steel Dragon tribute band called Blood Pollution. (Don't even get us started on those band names.) Members of Steel Dragon suddenly call on Izzy to replace their lead singer. This is every teenage boy's fantasy. Hell, this is every forty-year-old man's fantasy: photocopier technician one day, rock star the next.

Getting to be the new lead singer for your favorite band is an amazing opportunity. But what Izzy found is that just because you "sound like" someone, it doesn't mean you are a rock star. In fact, imitating an original comes with its own set of challenges. How many cover songs can you remember that are actually better than the original? Not many.

We have seen this play out in real life with people like Arnel Pineda, who went from living in poverty in the Philippines to touring the world as the lead singer for Journey. Even though you can close your eyes, listen to him, and hear echoes of Steve Perry, he is no more than a copy of the original. Imitation doesn't require courage, innovation, risk, or vision. Truth is, it's way easier to mimic someone else than it is to discover what *you* really sound like. But with limited risk comes limited reward.

The legends of rock 'n' roll have such identifiable voices that it only takes a few bars of a song before you know exactly who is singing. Whether it's Axl Rose of Guns N' Roses, Steven Tyler of Aerosmith, Prince, Michael Jackson, or Adele, when these singers open their mouths, you can immediately identify the band or act. These are all examples of iconic, original voices that have inspired imitation over and over again.

Finding your Own Original Voice (OOV) is a journey, one that takes time. Even the Beatles honored those who inspired them, but John Lennon never made it his business to sound like Elvis. Instead, he drew on Elvis's influence as he pursued becoming himself. Drawing from your influences while also developing your own perspective allows your voice to stand out from the crowd of imitators.

Two-time Grammy Award winner Tom Waits has a voice once described as "sounding like it was soaked in a vat of bourbon, left hanging in the smokehouse for a few months, and then taken outside and run over with a car." Who could ever forget that description? Rock stars develop a voice that is worth remembering. They find a unique way of expressing themselves that goes far beyond "typical" and connects with people in a much deeper way. Rock icons inspire growth in their listeners, encouraging them to develop their OOV in life.

ROCK STARS OF CHANGE: JIM KNIGHT

Author/speaker and culture catalyst Jim Knight developed his OOV over a twenty-one-year career with the legendary brand Hard Rock International. From his early days as a staff-level host at Hard Rock Cafe to becoming the senior director of training and development, Jim relished the fact that Hard Rock embraced individuality. His belief in an "army of diversity" allowed him not only to find his OOV but also to encourage the same discovery for those he trained.

In the long list of big changes that have happened in Jim Knight's life, he can honestly say that all of it was "intended" change. He admits good luck and being securely grounded are reasons why the big shifts were positive and by design.

"Whether it was getting married, having kids, accepting Christ in my life, taking on jobs, buying property, etc., all of it was intended," says Knight. "I have never been fired from a job or stayed too long at a job I did not like. I took my time and got married later in life, and I grew up in a positive, faith-based environment. It sounds like Nirvana, but I truly have not had the same struggles that many of my friends have experienced with unexpected change."

It was that deliberate intention that drove Knight to leave a very successful twenty-one-year career in training and development with Hard Rock International to pursue becoming a professional speaker and author.

He reflects, "I had always dreamed of being a performer . . . and speaking in front of a large group turned out to be a real strength for me. Once I identified that, I knew that Hard Rock would be the perfect opening act to my ultimate headlining career of being a keynote speaker and author."

It was a risky move, but it paid off. Knight's book, *Culture That Rocks*, has become a bestseller, and he has emerged as one of the foremost thought leaders on company culture and service. But his rise to the top of the speaker's circuit had humble beginnings.

"When I first started to speak on the side, during my time with Hard Rock, I only spoke about the brand, its storied history, and the learnings derived from that rock 'n' roll oriented environment," he remembers. "These paid speeches were just variations on a theme of what we would normally teach in a new hire orientation to new employees joining Hard Rock. Audiences loved the irreverent, rock-inspired story, and most attendees were able to make the connection of what I was teaching to the issues their specific brand was going through."

The "cover songs" he was teaching included well-known platforms, like Stephen Covey's *The Seven Habits of Highly Effective People*. However, as Knight got better in his delivery, he noticed that audiences desired a more customized approach to the content, rather than just hearing about Hard Rock examples.

"I began to weave in my own beliefs, observations, stories, and alternative brand analogies into my paid sessions," he tells us. "I still relied on the Hard Rock content as the anchor to my presentations, but by including an equal mix of personal stories and non-industry examples, I received better feedback and higher ratings. Additionally, as I adjusted my content, I amped up my delivery style. I purposefully studied other speakers and their delivery to see what elements I could incorporate that would make the most sense for me."

The more Knight facilitated sessions, the more he developed his OOV. As his style and approach became more authentic, he saw more opportunities present themselves.

"As my career progressed, I noticed that audiences gravitated more toward my unique concepts and delivery method, which has a little bit of rock 'n' roll infused throughout. I discovered that the only way to truly make a living as a professional speaker is to possess both great content and stellar delivery. You cannot just have one or the other. Today, facilitators have to be 'edutaining,' that is, they have to create the perfect mix of education and entertainment. I discovered my OOV by creating my own original content and style," explains Knight.

On whether there was a compelling reason or event that made him go his own way, he remarks, "The main reason why I decided to 'retire' from corporate life and do my own thing was about bigger impact and influence in the world. After twenty-one years, I felt like I had done everything I could do with a fantastic brand; I had won the highest awards in most Training & Development categories, my team was poised to keep the trajectory going, and the brand was in a positive place. Although working for an international, growth-focused, music-oriented organization like Hard Rock was the pinnacle in the hospitality industry . . . it wasn't enough. I wanted more. I aspired to do my own thing and add my unique 'voice' to the global party. I had bold thoughts and ideas that I wanted to share with any and every leader, and I realized that I would have to step away from the brand."

By finding his OOV, Jim now offers a completely unique perspective on organizational culture. So much so, that his book *Culture That Rocks: How to Revolutionize Your Company's Culture* has already sold thousands of copies. Jim is now one of the country's most-requested thought leaders on organizational culture, world-class service, employee branding and engagement, and performance management.

Although it might not be the way in which he intended, Jim Knight is, without a doubt, a complete rock star. And it started by developing his OOV, one that is unique and relevant to his mission.

3. Rock Stars Are on the Front Lines of Creating Something New

Voltaire once said, "Our wretched species is so made that those who walk on the well-trodden path always throw stones at those who are showing a new road." With every new song written, rock stars, by virtue of their job description, are innovators. But by sharing their songs with the world, they open themselves up to criticism.

SPEAKING OF CRITICISM, "WHOA, THAT WAS REALLY SOMETHING"; "HEY, MAN, YOU DID YOUR THING"; AND, "THAT WAS REALLY INTERESTING," ARE NICE WAYS IN WHICH FELLOW MUSICIANS INDICATE THAT WHAT YOU JUST DID SUCKED.

To be a true original is rare. Hell, it is damned near impossible. Even Picasso said, "Good artists copy; great artists steal." Innovation is about expansion and is best when done with a deep regard for the shoulders on which the "would-be" innovator stands.

We are not asking you to go into a cave in search of that which never existed. What we are asking is for you to manifest your personal mission by understanding what "is" while working toward what could be. When we are faced with change, we are always staring at something new. So, in essence, the change we face is our chance to create. And, without getting too preachy, we believe an inherent joy comes from imitating our creator by simply endeavoring to create.

Dave Evans is a name you might not be familiar with. We're not quite sure how to say this, but Dave is kind of a big deal. The story goes that he responded to a note left on the Mount Temple Comprehensive School bulletin board in the fall of 1976. The note was an ad, looking for anyone interested in starting a band. The band formed from that note is still together, over forty years later. That band is U2, and Dave Evans is better known as "The Edge."

Bono gave Dave his famous moniker due to his "sharp mind and the way he always observed things from the edge." That point of view is probably why he single-handedly revolutionized how guitar players use "echo." For decades, the echo was used subtly, in the background, by guitarists to create a lush, full sound. It was never intended to be front and center. That is, until The Edge made it just that.

Immortalized in the classic song "Where the Streets Have No Name" and highlighted in the rock documentary *It Might Get Loud*, this echo became something completely new as The Edge responded to the innate urge to create. He made the echo fill in notes that he wasn't playing—as if there were two guitars being played. In his own words, "I could see ways to use it that had never been used. Suddenly, everything changed."

Everything suddenly changed, even for one of the most respected guitarists in rock 'n' roll. The Edge has been referred to as the "anti-guitar hero," due to his lack of blistering, over-indulgent guitar solos. However, his desire to create something new has led to his technically undemanding yet completely original sound. While most modern guitarists are using tiny pedal boards to generate sounds, one look at The Edge's monstrous guitar rig (the size of a refrigerator) shows just how much he values innovation. It also illustrates just how much this generation of gunslingers is chasing him—wannabe rock stars imitating a real one. The Edge's compulsion to be on the front lines of creating something new is one of the reasons this rock star is in the Hall of Fame and why true Rock Stars of Change seek the equivalent.

4. Rock Stars Have Enough Swagger to Carry Them through Difficult Times

When he first started making music, record labels constantly turned down Grammy-winning, multi-million-album-selling recording artist Ed Sheeran. Sheeran jokes that he was "slightly chubby and a ginger"—and that wasn't "marketable" for record labels. Can you say, *Wrong*?! Sheeran has two of the biggest-selling albums of the millennium and plays to sold-out arenas all over the world.

A rock star's road to success is paved with years of playing poorly promoted shows, crashing on couches, driving through the night, and eating gas station hot dogs. Facing difficult times doesn't mean you throw in the towel. Towel throwing is not part of a rock star's skill set—unless it's soaked in sweat and tossed to a clamoring fan—nor should it be for you.

Sheeran has been described as "confident without being cocky, polite without being a pushover, and intelligent but unpretentious." That could serve as the definition of what is known in the music business as *swagger*.

We used to think that being a rock star was 90 percent swagger and 10 percent talent, as evidenced by some of the leather-clad heroes of the 80s. Giant hair and an exposed chest seemed to be enough to overcome even the harshest of critics or weakest of lyrics. But, in reality, misplaced confidence is a dangerous form of ignorance. A true rock star has enough confidence to overcome difficult times. However, he is also grounded in truth. He doesn't ignore facts because they disagree with him or make up "facts" to support his narrative. His confidence stems from years of preparedness that have carried him to this point.

It was preparedness that allowed Keni Thomas and the 3rd Ranger Battalion to achieve rock-star status. Here is their story, as told by National Geographic channel:

A team of U.S. Rangers surrounds a building in the heart of rebel-held Mogadishu, Somalia, in 1993. Under rebel fire, the Rangers have captured two of Mohamed Farrah Aidid's top lieutenants and are about to head back to their base camp when they hear over the radio: "Black Hawk down." Just then, they watch as the helicopter barrels toward the ground, falling behind the horizon. "A moment later I could hear the impact," U.S. Ranger Randy Ramaglia says, "and that changed the entire mission."What was supposed to be a one-hour "snatch-and-grab" job has now turned into a rescue mission. Seconds after the crash, their squad leader is shot in the neck and is bleeding badly. Ranger Keni Thomas is immediately thrust into the leadership role and has to guide his team to the crash site. They know from past experience that the only chance their comrades have to stay alive depends on reaching them before the rebels do[2].

While facing a situation of intense change, Thomas found confidence in his training. He says, "Leadership has never been about the rank or the position you hold. It's about the example you set. People to your left and right are counting on you, and it's up to you to deliver. But you will only be as good as you prepared yourself to be."

Mike Durant was piloting one of the Black Hawk helicopters that day. As he hovered above the fighting, his helicopter was shot down. The rebels then captured him. It wasn't until the news report appeared on television that Mike's fellow rangers realized he was alive and had been captured. The Ranger's creed doesn't allow for a fallen brother to be left behind. The Rangers immediately returned to the city and enlisted the help of negotiators to secure Mike's safe release.

It may seem odd to suggest that Thomas and his battalion had swagger at the Battle of Mogadishu. But it's that confidence that gives others something to hold on to. It's that confidence that allowed Mike Durant to believe he wouldn't be left behind. Keni Thomas and the 3rd Ranger Battalion are real-life rock stars. In fact, Thomas is now a successful speaker and recording artist. His band, Cornbread, was featured in the Reese Witherspoon movie *Sweet Home Alabama*.

RISK 'N' ROLL: ORIGINALITY MATTERS

The history of rock 'n' roll is a memoir of risk, of daring to do something fresh and new. We see that a strong, original voice compels others to listen. When a rock star finds her OOV, she begins to build a solid foundation on which she can stand firm and drive change. The stronger our foundation, the more we develop our confidence, which allows us to be agile during difficult times and to face change with optimism and self-assurance.

The rock stars we have highlighted in this chapter all have a unique personal mission. A mission or desire to drive change is born from deeply held values and is not swayed by feelings in the moment, reaction from critics, or challenging circumstances.

---

[2]Sarah Beauchamp, "Survivors Recount the Harrowing 'Black Hawk Down' Story," *The Daily Beast*.

HELLO, SELF! HOW AM I DOING TONIGHT?

THE VALUE OF VALUES

Ancient history indicates a universal morality that has woven its way through time and culture. From the Code of Hammurabi to the Ten Commandments, the US Constitution, and the Mosaic Code, tribes and nations have used detailed moral statements as a way of clarifying what matters and why. Morality, in many respects, indicates what we should engage in and abstain from, but it can be best understood as the outward manifestation of our values. We use the term value to indicate what something is worth. A pre-CBS, vintage Fender Stratocaster is worth about twenty-five-thousand dollars and, therefore, is considered very valuable. The 1983 Hondo II student guitar your father bought for seventy-five dollars that hangs on your office wall is worth far more than twenty-five-thousand dollars to you but worth virtually nothing to anyone else.

While a standard of morality has been widely accepted throughout history, individual core values are unique and not necessarily appreciated by others; in other words, values are not universal. Instead, they are determined through a myriad of factors, including where we come from; our upbringing; our personal experiences; and the values of our parents, mentors, peer group, and the like. When we talk about values, we are talking about the deeply rooted characteristics, precepts, and practices that govern the way we live.

As Brant tells us, "When I was a kid, all I dreamed of was playing professional baseball. My life was centered around it. I had built a reputation of dominance as a pitcher. I was supposed to be the 'next big thing' to come out of Manchester, New Hampshire, following in the footsteps of my idol, Baltimore Orioles legend Mike Flanagan.

"I come from a baseball family. My father is a well-known pitching coach who has worked with two Cy Young award winners and several world champions. My uncle was a highly recruited catcher for the

University of New Haven before becoming a successful high school and college coach. Baseball is in my blood. I remember standing on the mound, even as young as twelve years old, taunting batters to step to the plate and face me. I thrived on the competition and lived the famous words of Ricky Bobby: 'If you ain't first, you're last.'

"When I was fifteen, I was playing in the state semi-final soccer game for Manchester Memorial High School. I was a striker (big surprise), and in the fourth quarter, I found myself with a breakaway to the goal, with only one person to beat. It was a freezing November evening with wind chills in the negative-ten-degree range. As I approached the goal, I relished the situation I was in. One on one: heaven on earth to me.

"I had my plan. I would fake right, burst left, and bury the ball in the lower left net. I made my move and then . . . change. The opposing player went to slide tackle me and missed the ball entirely. He caught both my legs and sent me into an aerial somersault. I couldn't get my hands out to break my fall, and I landed violently between my head and shoulder. Crack! That's all I heard. My right arm was numb—my pitching arm. I couldn't move it as I had suffered a gruesome third-degree AC joint separation to my shoulder that nearly broke the skin. As they gently pulled my shirt off, I heard a gasp from the stands. All I could think about was baseball.

"Standing in the freezing cold, I felt my entire future running away. After receiving emergency care and having a few weeks of healing under my belt, I went to see the first orthopedic doctor I could. He took one look at me and said very bluntly, 'You probably will never pitch again.' In that six-word sentence, he stole 100 percent of my hope. I had a mountain of rehabilitation to climb, and this guy just made it the heights of Everest. Even though I couldn't hold half a pound out in front me at the time, I continued to push through.

"We were able to get in touch with my father's old student and my hero Mike Flanagan, who made an appointment for us with the Red Sox team physician, Dr. Arthur Pappas. He looked at my arm and the x-rays and told me I would definitely throw again, but I wouldn't throw as hard as I once did. In fact, there was a good chance, if I proceeded with surgery, that I would develop severe arthritis before age thirty. But he encouraged me to continue with rehab and to see what happened. Even though he had difficult news to deliver, he did it in an empathetic way that didn't destroy the dreams of a teenage boy. As I write this today, as a forty-five-year-old man with an awful memory, I can still recall that moment as clear as day. The impact of these events is why hope and empathy are two of my core values, and these values still drive me, thirty years after suffering my injury."

Values help us align things, like how we should behave and who we truly want to be. Organizations use values to determine everything from whom they should hire to the foundation their culture should be built on. If we don't identify our foundational values, then our ability to make sound decisions and stand in the face of adversity will shift with the wind. Depending on how hard the wind is blowing, this can lead to destructive and dangerous results. Our values serve as shelter to protect us from life's storms, and the protection they offer isn't limited to ourselves. It is extended to those who are close to us, those we love, and sometimes, even, those we inspire.

War and Peace author Leo Tolstoy is remembered for a number of things—including his values. Considered one of the greatest writers in history, his life and work have transcended his own time. The reach and quality of Tolstoy's writing have prompted scholarly exposition as to whom the man behind the pen really was, and the results are as fascinating as his books.

Tolstoy was at once both inspired and tortured. We have spoken about vulnerability as a great strength, and transparency and vulnerability were powerful motivating values for this man, who shared with the world his desperate need to understand the meaning of life. While he may be most famous for his works of fiction, his nonfiction writings reflect the depth of his curiosity and the life he endeavored to live in light of his conclusions.

Nonviolence, temperance, and the avoidance of lust and anger are values that ripple through his writing. An ardent proponent of vegetarianism, his views were an extension of his pacifism and desire for peace:

Flesh eating is simply immoral, as it involves the performance of an act which is contrary to moral feeling: By killing, man suppresses in himself, unnecessarily, the highest spiritual capacity, that of sympathy and pity toward living creatures like himself and by violating his own feelings becomes cruel . . . As long as there are slaughterhouses, there will be battlefields.

What we discover in considering the life and work of Leo Tolstoy is that when our core values are ignored, hidden, or compromised, we not only suffer as individuals but as a people. Conversely, when we proclaim our truth, while courageously and unapologetically modeling it, our potential impact is limitless.

Tolstoy's impact on Mahatma Gandhi has been widely documented. While correspondence between the two indicates camaraderie and commiseration, the beginning of Gandhi and Tolstoy's relationship was, in essence, a fan letter from a man who would eventually lead the peaceful revolution that freed the people of India from Great Britain's oppressive rule.

Fifty-plus years after Tolstoy's death and nearly six thousand miles away, the Rev. Dr. Martin Luther King Jr. was fighting for the civil rights of his fellow Americans. King's appreciation for Tolstoy was unabashed. From personal writings to public speeches, King credited Tolstoy as one of his single-greatest influences. Who else made Dr. King's list? If you guessed the Tolstovian fan boy Mahatma Gandhi, you got it right.

Tolstoy's existential crisis and convictions could have gone with him to his grave. He could have, out of fear and self-doubt, kept his thoughts to himself. His desire for impact could have been numbed by cultural norms, and he could have applied a myriad of excuses to justify his silence. Thankfully, however, Leo Tolstoy was a man of deep conviction. At the heart of his purpose was a values-soaked desire for change and a quest for truth. We find that one's level of fulfillment is inextricably linked to his life's purpose and values.

VALUES + PURPOSE = FULFILLMENT

As we said earlier, we develop our values over the course of our lives. A detailed exploration of your values and an assessment of the extent to which those values are being honored will reveal the challenges you are facing and serve as the prescription for what is ailing you. When we live a life in line with our values, it helps us decide what our life's purpose should be.

Purpose is a well-documented subject that has entire methodologies built around it. Whether it's Rick Warren's *Purpose Driven Life* or Dick Bolles's *What Color is Your Parachute?* you could read a book a day for a year and still not get through them all. Many of them talk about "finding" your life's purpose. After a discussion with Susan Shea, ED. S., we believe we don't actually "find" our purpose; we choose it. Susan explains choice, values, and purpose:

> The science of human behavior explains how and why people behave and regulate their lives in certain ways. In short, what we choose to do or not do and how we feel about what we do is determined by our history. Our experiences and learning determine not only our behavior but also what we value and don't value. And our values determine how we feel about what we do and don't do in the world. There is no intrinsic purpose motivating us along our life's path. The science is way more fascinating and revelatory than stories we've made up about it. Scientific evidence shows us that we can have a massive influence on our own behavior and in creating outcomes for ourselves. We determine how to intervene in our own lives. We choose our values, and those values shape and ultimately determine what we call our life's purpose. So, if you want to know your purpose, science informs us to stop searching for it and start creating it. Our unique ability to choose the

values we live by is one of the things that makes human beings such a powerful and creative force in the world.

This is an empowering thought on the importance of defining our values and using them to help make the choices in our lives that will drive the impact we are looking to make. Identifying and living by what we value is a process that requires focus and discipline, as we can be thwarted by how we are feeling in the moment.

Often, when we face stressful emotions, like fear, disappointment, dissatisfaction, and desperation, what we "value" may shift temporarily. A word of caution: sometimes this shift in values is predicated by unwanted change. It's the diehard atheist who prays when his life is on the line or the couch potato who starts going to the gym after learning she has diabetes. We must be aware of the circumstances we are facing in the moment and the impact they are having on our choices.

SOMETIMES IT TAKES UNWANTED CHANGE TO GET US TO MEANINGFULLY ENGAGE CORE VALUES THAT HAVE BEEN IGNORED.

If we allow things like fear, disappointment, and desperation to guide our choices, we are placing our feelings and emotions in the driver's seat. Feelings and emotions are unreliable drivers.

SEPARATING VALUES FROM FEELINGS

In spite of what the classic Morris Albert song suggests, "Feelings" are much more than "nothing." They are powerful motivators for making decisions. However, feelings change, and are, therefore, unreliable tools for making good decisions.

Remember that time you were so in love with your "soul mate" that the tattoo you got in her honor lasted longer than the actual relationship? Well, that was a bad idea motivated by a good feeling. Feelings are not the enemy and actually serve an important role in the process of change. However, they cannot be the primary factor when making decisions.

Self-awareness is an essential tool for accurately understanding the cause and potential impact of our feelings. By allowing us to see how we "feel" about the change we are engaging, we are able to honestly identify our level of commitment. If we value our health enough to go to the gym on Monday, but then wake up "feeling" tired on Tuesday, we have a choice to make. Does our value surrounding health win? Or does the feeling of exhaustion put our supposed core value in the passenger seat? Change is easy when our feelings are aligned with our values. It's the common tug of war between the two that makes change often feel impossible.

ROCK STARS OF CHANGE: ALAN SCHAEFER

But remember, change doesn't understand impossible. Just ask Alan Schaefer, CEO/Founder of Banding People Together. We have all heard the occasional story of someone going from rags to riches to rags. But how often does that experience lead to the development of a wildly successful consulting organization?

In 1993, twin brothers and musicians, Alan and Robert Schaefer, had a completely original idea. They wanted to post their band's tour schedule on this thing called the "internet." Even though they were told the internet was just a "fad," Alan took his sales and marketing prowess and Robert his coding expertise, and they pushed forward with the development of what became tourdates.com. It wasn't long before their tiny, two-man shop received a buy-out offer . . . for eight figures. Yes, you read that right, eight figures. Two "band guys" just became overnight millionaires. This allowed them to pursue their first love, music, with reckless abandon. That is, until they lost eight figures nearly as quickly as they made it.

The company that acquired tourdates.com was acquired by another organization that reorganized, leaving the Schaefer brothers with not much more than the worthless paper their stock options were written on. They took what little cash they had received in the deal and paid off debts before deciding to continue their pursuit of music. Their band, Five Star Iris, had a respectable amount of success, with nationwide airplay, favorable write-ups in trade magazines, and a world tour, including playing in seventeen countries for our troops.

It was during that time that Alan, the quintessential lead singer, was having trouble with his band mates. Their goals and the effort needed to reach them were most certainly not in alignment amongst the band members. It was about that time that a friend and successful CEO recommended that Alan read a book by renowned author Patrick Lencioni entitled *Five Dysfunctions of a Team*. It is a leadership fable that has become required reading for most executives.

After reading the book, Alan realized he wasn't leading the band effectively and became obsessed with becoming a better collaborator. Fast-forward a few years and the countless hours of research and endless pursuit of collaborative utopia has created his latest organization, Banding People Together. Banding People Together combines behavioral science and rock 'n' roll to produce high-performing organizations. They do this through experiential workshops, their own scientifically developed methodology, and consulting.

Needless to say, going from a catamaran in the British Virgin Islands to living off credit cards while building a completely original consulting practice has presented some seriously difficult change for the former rock star.

Alan notes, "After letting go of the illusion that I was supposed to be on the cover of *Rolling Stone*, I started Banding People Together to help people work together in a way that felt more human. Unfortunately, I wasn't really practicing what I preached. Because of that, I wasn't an effective leader. The most difficult change I went through was becoming a leader worth following. I wasn't setting other up for success, and I wasn't facing issues head-on. I blamed others and allowed myself to spend countless hours pointing fingers, instead of taking responsibility."

One of the main focuses of a Banding People Together workshop is self-awareness, which happens to be a key component of successful change. Learning how you choose to collaborate with others is revealing, but understanding how others choose to work with you is enlightening. Becoming a better collaborator (or change-maker) requires you to become vulnerable enough to ask yourself some difficult questions and courageous enough to live with the answers.

It was within that very process that Alan found the solutions he was searching for: "I simply had to get honest with myself. Luckily, I had some people who were willing to invest in me to help me see others and myself differently. I had to make very difficult decisions and realize that things would get worse before they got better."

As we now know, intentional change can produce unexpected con- sequences. Making intentional decisions allowed Alan to move the organization forward, but it was another realization that truly allowed the company to flourish. Alan reflects, "I was more impacted by the decisions I didn't make. The unexpected consequences showed up in poor performance, stress, and inconsistent results. The worst consequence was that I was being negatively impacted in a way that made me show up in a way for my wife that wasn't healthy or fair to her. So, I simply started making better decisions, and the perceived 'problems' went away quickly."

Just as we mentioned earlier, if we try to ignore change and pretend it's not happening, it can become an unruly houseguest in our lives. In fact, the repercussions of not dealing with it can bleed into the relationships we hold dearest, even when those relationships have nothing to do with the actual change we are facing. Having the awareness to realize when that is happening can free us from days, weeks, and even months of unnecessary turmoil. It becomes a central competency of any aspiring entrepreneur.

As Alan continued to learn and allowed himself to be mentored, he was able to develop a distinct viewpoint that has enabled him to become one of the preeminent thought leaders around collaboration and effective communication. Alan concludes that the ups and downs of creating something new have much to offer when it comes to valuable takeaways: "I just kept letting myself evolve with each venture I tried. I would process the 'learns,' the things I could control, as well as things I realized I couldn't control, and I combined that with wisdom from others. It was like compounded interest that was additive over time, until one day, out of nowhere, I had a voice that the world was identifying with."

That voice now leads the only consultancy of its kind on the planet—an organization that uses music as a Trojan horse for a bunch of behavioral science that allows collaboration to be taught, developed, measured, and repeated within any organization. This becomes the central engine to drive any successful change initiative.

If anyone truly embodies the "rock 'n' roll with it" approach, it is, quite literally, Alan Schaefer.

SUPPORTIVE AND UNSUPPORTIVE FEELINGS

For the purposes of change, we will place our feelings in two categories: supportive and unsupportive. We are careful not to judge feelings as "good" or "bad" as our unsupportive feelings often exist for good reason. If, for example, past trauma, abuse, or a medical condition causes our unsupportive feelings, then they deserve to be honored. Supportive feelings might at first seem scarce, but often increase with results. By understanding the role feelings play in our ability to engage change, we are able to revel in feelings that move us closer to the goal line while preemptively identifying the unsupportive feelings that are bound to get in our way. It is a game changer, for many of us, to understand that we can consider and direct our feelings.

Feelings are a major part of our inner narrative. We laugh at *Saturday Night Live*'s Stuart Smalley when he looks in the mirror, reciting his affirmation: "I'm good enough, I'm smart enough, and doggonit, people like me." While his character is, indeed, funny, the work of reprogramming our self-talk is serious business. Feelings fuel the direction of how we talk to ourselves. How many times have you made a mistake? Or felt embarrassed? Or said something like, "I am so stupid"? Now consider how you would talk to a child who made a mistake.

Imagine if your eight-year-old little girl spills a glass of juice or has a hard time with her spelling homework. She, too, may feel embarrassed. It would do serious damage, on many levels, if, in that moment, you call her stupid. She is more likely to continue to engage when she is met with phrases like, "It's okay. We all make mistakes"; "I know you did your best"; or, "I bet you'll get better the more you try." You are no different.

In chapter 1, we referenced the engraftment process when speaking of Theo's bone marrow transplant. During this process, your body is at the highest risk of infection until the cells engraft. You are at your most vulnerable, so for protection, the doctors place you in a "clean room," which has positive pressure at all times. This means the air in the room is constantly blowing out and not being recycled. This provides the safest environment for the patient. Everyone who enters the room must wear a gown, gloves, and mask to ensure the space is not contaminated.

In the process of change, negative self-talk acts like an aggressive infection, waiting for a vulnerable moment to attack and do the most damage. We must do our best to place ourselves in a "clean room" and surround ourselves with supportive feelings to fend off any potential threats and make it through the waiting period before our own change engrafts.

We are not asking you to wear a pastel, argyle sweater vest or get a ridiculous haircut a la Stuart Smalley—unless you already have those things, in which case, we don't judge. What we are suggesting is the following: be aware of how you respond to your own mistakes and feelings; pause before you respond to yourself; when you do respond, think about how you would communicate with a child who really wants to do well. Many of us were raised with the golden rule of treating others the way you want to be treated. But we have a new rule for you: treat yourself the way you want others to treat you.

To help you identify your feelings, we have included a list of common feelings—both supportive and unsupportive. Keep in mind, this is not an exhaustive list, and we encourage you to be as specific as you can be. Later in the book, we will provide a step-by-step process to navigating change, and you can use this list as a reference to help pinpoint what you are feeling.

SUPPORTIVE FEELINGS

Affectionate	Empowered	Joyful	Refreshed
Amazed	Excited	Loved	Renewed
Appreciative	Exuberant	Liberated	Restored
Amused	Fulfilled	Lucky	Revived
Brave	Free	Moved	Satisfied
Blissful	Fortunate	Mellow	Surprised
Calm	Grateful	Optimistic	Safe
Confident	Happy	Peaceful	Stimulated
Content	Invigorated	Pleased	Sympathetic
Compassionate	Involved	Proud	Thankful
Comfortable	Impulsive	Passionate	Trusted
Curious	Interested	Relaxed	
Encouraged	Inspired	Relieved	

UNSUPPORTIVE FEELINGS

Abandoned	Embarrassed	Mocked	Unknown
Alone	Fearful	Neglected	Unimportant
Ashamed	Hungry	Offended	Uniformed
Brushed off	Humiliated	Put down	Unloved
Beaten down	Ignored	Rejected	Unsupported
Confused	Insignificant	Resentful	Unwanted
Cut down	Inferior	Ridiculed	Uncared for
Criticized	Insulted	Stereotyped	Unapproved
Disapproved	Invalidated	Stifled	Unaware
Discouraged	Labeled	Teased	Unable
Dehumanized	Lectured to	Threatened	Worthless
Disrespected	Lonely	Underestimated	
Exhausted	Misunderstood	Unheard	

So, how do we separate our values from our feelings? We'd rather you don't! Our feelings help us know when we are acting in alignment with our values. By understanding the difference between supportive and unsupportive feelings, we are able to bridle our inner narrative, identify challenges, and keep the commitments we make in service of our goals. The more honest and connected we are to what we are feeling, the less likely we are to stray from walking our values-based path.

IDENTIFYING OUR VALUES

Identifying personal values is like panning for gold. It is an intentional endeavor that requires focus, effort, and patience. We need to sift through lots of relationships, memories, and experiences to find the nuggets that mean the most. The beauty of this process is the guaranteed gold at the end of the expedition—but only if we do things the right way. The gold we find will be instrumental in successfully coping with and conquering the change we face. Later, we will provide a detailed worksheet for you to walk through and identify your core values. But let's talk now about the process we will use.

How do we identify our specific values? Values can be hidden in what psychologist Abraham Maslow refers to as "peak experiences." Those are the moments when we experience deep satisfaction, groundedness, and strength. Dissecting those moments and the circumstances present in those memories can aid in revealing that which we hold most dear. Can you think of a specific time when you felt like you were on top of the world? What led you to feel that way? Diving into those experiences is an excellent way to identify what matters to you personally.

We can also find values in the relationships we have with the people we most admire. What is it that attracts us to them? Why do we hold this relationship in such high regard? What are the characteristics we want to imitate?

Jim shares with us, "I was moved the first time I stepped into a river to fly fish with Al. He asked me to pause so that he could remember his friends who had gone before and express gratitude that he is still here. The man who taught me to fly fish and tie my own flies was, at the same time, teaching me how to live. At eighty-seven years old, Al Seavy is still wading wild rivers on his own, living with inspirational joy and depth.

"For Al, a trout stream is a metaphor for life. He explains that the surface of a river moves at a faster pace than it does at its bed, due to the boulders and trees that have fallen and sunk to the bottom over the years. His point is that we all have boulders and fallen timber in our memories, and we need to make sure they don't slow us down.

"Al is the kind of guy who drinks Chock Full o' Nuts coffee because it's what he's been drinking for seventy years. He sticks with what works. I've seen him spend half a day trying to catch one fish and correcting me for wanting to move on. As Al says, 'Never leave fish to find fish.' Gratitude, simplicity, joy, adventure, a love of nature, and a commitment to good health are values that I hold dear and endeavor to imitate as lived out by this dear friend and mentor."

Even our favorite character from a book or movie can help us identify our values. What was it about the individual that inspired you? Where in your own life would you like to be like him? What about his story would you like to experience? Identifying what we are attracted to brings us closer to having an open and honest conversation with ourselves about the values closest to our hearts.

Creative visualization is another method for discovering deeply held values. In the cult-classic Adam Sandler movie Happy Gilmore, the hockey player turned golfer learns to go to his personal "happy place" when he needs to settle himself and focus. He finds a sense of calmness in his grandmother, wearing a Gene Simmons mask (from KISS), his scantily clad girlfriend holding two pitchers of beer, and a little person dressed as a cowboy riding through his visualization. Again, no judgment from us and a very rock 'n' roll way to do things!

To help you identify what you truly value, we have included a list of common values for you to look over. Values are very personal; thus, you might not find your exact values on any pre-made list. We encourage you to make this personal. Dig deep. Take a moment and look over these words. Are there any that stand out or that you connect with immediately? Circle them and come back to this page when you begin your worksheet in the last chapter. Are there any you might add?

AUTHENTICITY	ACHIEVEMENT	ADVENTURE	AUTHORITY
AUTONOMY	BALANCE	BOLDNESS	COMPASSION
CHALLENGE	CITIZENSHIP	COMMUNITY	COMPETENCY
COLLABORATION	CREATIVITY	CURIOSITY	DETERMINATION
FAIRNESS	FAITH	FAME	FRIENDSHIPS
FUN	GROWTH	HAPPINESS	HARMONY
HONESTY	HUMOR	INFLUENCE	INTEGRITY
JUSTICE	KINDNESS	KNOWLEDGE	LEADERSHIP
LEARNING	LOVE	LOYALTY	OPTIMISM
PEACE	PLEASURE	RECOGNITION	RESPECT
RESPONSIBILITY	SECURITY	SELF-RESPECT	SERVICE
SPIRITUALITY	STABILITY	SUCCESS	TRUST

The most powerful changes are born from our values while honoring our feelings. This work requires a level of vulnerability, courage, and honesty that many will never engage. Remember, one of the key characteristics of a rock star is being willing to take risks. For those who will go to this place, the potential power and impact is transformational. If we truly want to change, identifying our values and understanding our feelings are non-negotiable exercises.

LET'S GO "CRAISY!"

UNINTENTIONAL VS. INTENTIONAL CHANGE

Remember, change in and of itself is not intrinsically good or bad. It just is. You could win the lottery, find a new job, lose a loved one, travel overseas, or even take the giant risk of starting your own company. As you can see, in each of these examples, change has many faces. For our purposes, we are going to focus specifically on two areas of change:

1. Unintentional change
2. Intentional change

The previous examples of change fall into one of these two categories. Unintentional and intentional changes are intertwined together, seamlessly flowing into one another like yin and yang.

When Harold Mantius began working as an engineer for Ocean Spray, one of the first things he noticed was they discarded the husks, or outer skin, of the cranberries. Tons of leftover husks were literally the unintentional result of extracting the juice concentrate from the cranberries. Traditionally, these byproducts were gathered and sold as cattle feed. In doing so, Ocean Spray made pennies on the dollar. Mantius knew there had to be a better and more profitable use for these husks. He was right. Mantius is the inventor of what we now know as Craisins®, which are now one of the most successful products in the Ocean Spray family. In fact, they are so popular that the company now has an extreme excess of cranberry extract due to the demand for Craisins.

This is a perfect example of how unintentional change converted into intentional change, eventually resulting in the Craisin. Interestingly, the overwhelming success of the Craisin has now created an additional unintentional change—the overage of cranberry extract. Now the engineers and innovators at Ocean Spray need to convert this unintentional change into something intentional. The cycle continues to spin, with new products now on the horizon.

When faced with unintentional change, we can heighten our defense mechanisms, due to the perceived threat of uncertainty. Our response to the unexpected ultimately determines our level of success in achieving our goal of converting it to intentional change.

Jim remembers heading home from a family vacation one summer: "We stopped for lunch and noticed an elderly couple sitting next us. The woman leaned in and cut up her husband's meat, at which point we realized he was a stroke victim. With slurred speech and the use of one arm, he sat with his wife and ate his lunch. My father was distracted by them and leaned toward my mother and whispered, 'Theresa, if that ever happens to me, take me out in the back yard and shoot me.' We finished our lunch and drove home, with plans of spending the last day of vacation in Boston.

"James Ernest Trick was six-foot-four, wore size fourteen shoes, and had hands the size of small dogs. He was a powerful, imposing man who had spent twenty-two years serving as a chief in the United States Navy. My father carried that role and title into our home long after his retirement. He would often end sentences with the military phrase 'end of report.'

"'Dad, can I use the car tomorrow?' I'd ask. 'Who's going to be in it with you?' Permission would only be granted if he approved of my choice of friends. Dave McCormick was my long-haired, electric-guitar-playing friend, and if his name was mentioned as a potential passenger in my father's 1982 Ford Escort, the answer would be a swift no, followed by a very clear 'end of report.' If that was his final answer, there'd be no reason to ask again. In fact, I don't think any of us ever even spoke after an 'end of report' had been laid down.

"Dad started complaining of a headache shortly after arriving in Boston. An hour or so later, he was not feeling well and was very pale. We decided to head home. I was disappointed to be leaving so soon. Upon arrival at the train station, my mother and I watched as my father suffered a massive brainstem stroke. Our world was turned upside down in the blink of an eye. We were told he wouldn't live through the night. That narrative continued for a week. They then told us that he would never walk, speak, or breathe without a ventilator attached to a tracheostomy. We were told he would never eat again and would need a feeding tube."

From catastrophic health issues to flat tires, natural disasters to our lover leaving, sometimes the trouble we weren't ever looking for comes looking for us—a mortal enemy that barges in, sits down in our favorite chair, and guzzles our most-expensive scotch, all while ordering MMA pay-per-view on our television. Without warning or invitation, unintentional change can upset our apple cart, making it easy to immediately jump to the worst-case scenario. Once we allow panic to set in, one of two things happen: we react by freaking out, or we become paralyzed. However, both hysteria (sorry, Def Leppard) and panic (not Panic at the Disco) are ineffective tools for dealing with unintentional change.

In a 2016 *Huffington Post* article, Dr. Gail Gross makes the following observations about the brain under stress:

> When the body is under stress, it moves into survival mode, better known as the fight-or-flight syndrome. Under these conditions, the body prepares itself by overproducing the stress hormone cortisol. Then, cortisol goes to the brain and causes a slow-down in the process of the pre-frontal cortex, where you think critically and have your executive function. Therefore, the captain of your ship is no longer in control, and the amygdala, where the fight or flight syndrome and your emotions come from, gets larger and

takes over the controls. Finally, the hippocampus, where your learning and memory are found, temporarily narrows.[3]

We are biologically created. So, when faced with an emergency, we are often reactive. Critical thinking goes out the door. As a result, panic elicits a purely emotional response. We naturally cease to be thoughtful or grounded as we encounter danger.

Jim's father might have been afraid. Who wouldn't be? The key is what he decided to do with that fear. Maybe it was his Navy training, or maybe it was because he was a stubborn old SOB, but within a year, he walked with canes, spoke clearly, was off the ventilator, and could eat again. Though he was still left seriously disabled, he recovered far beyond anyone's expectations. He didn't let fear of the future thwart his intention to fight back.

The truth is, we determine what's possible when we respond with intention to unexpected change. Succumbing to a "reactive" state can produce the kind of counterproductive panic that often makes things worse. Because our brain views the uncertain as a threat, the immediate response to change is fear. Fear can lead to irrational thoughts and behavior. This places us in danger of allowing feelings to drive the bus, as we spoke of in the last chapter.

In contrast, successfully engaging unintentional change begins with the following:

1. **Determine the immediate threat level:** Does this require an urgent response? Breaking a guitar string on stage is a drag but is not the same as being diagnosed with a terminal illness. This step ensures we will not overreact or underreact.

2. **Assess the situation:** Gather as much information as you can. Determine the root cause and the context in which that cause exists. Only by understanding these two items can we effectively move on to the next step.

3. **Determine your options:** Determine what options (strategies) are suitable for addressing the situation. If someone is choking, the Heimlich maneuver needs to be applied immediately. If

[3] http://www.huffingtonpost.com/dr-gail-gross/staying-calm-during-an-em_b_7749812.html

someone is just coughing, applying that technique is not only inappropriate, but it could cause actual harm. In determining suitable options, we increase the likelihood of an effective response.

4. **Make a plan:** Like a map, your plan shows a plausible way to move you through your current situation toward the desired destination. A plan protects you from becoming overwhelmed and ineffective.

5. **Take action:** Act with deliberate intention. A plan is only as effective as its execution. Action requires a mix of commitment and flexibility. Laser focus on an action plan, without considering new information or unforeseen circumstances, can create dangerous blind spots.

Consider two other key points when facing unintentional change: First, become aware of potential speed bumps and potholes. Things like irrational fear, limited thinking, and negative self-talk have the potential to make us lose perspective. That loss of perspective starts a downward spiral that can be difficult to pull out of.

Second, ask for and be open to help. During difficult times, it is invaluable to have a network of close, trusted friends and family who can be direct and honest with you. Unintentional change can skew your ability to see clearly. You'll likely remain on target if you have people close to you who can recognize when you veer off path and call you to the carpet when needed.

Conversely, sometimes when we least expect it, complete strangers can provide the aid we need. It could come in a moment as serious as an assault or heart attack, or it could be as simple as asking a stranger for directions. In particular, men are known for not asking for help, but we must all be open to input and assistance when up against the unexpected.

Jim remembers clearly, "When my father had his brain stem stroke, both my mother and the train conductor implored my father to go immediately to the hospital. He declined, certain that he would be fine. By the time he was willing to ask, it was too late."

For many people like Jim's father, seeking the help of strangers equals weakness. Facing unexpected change requires us to trade insecurity for wisdom. The real challenge when facing unintentional change is responding with deliberate intention. The chance of pulling out of a downward spiral is severely diminished when we react by just "winging it," rather than responding with a plan.

ROCK STARS OF CHANGE: THE SHEEHY'S

To illustrate our point, consider our interview with one of the bravest families we have ever met: the Sheehys. Megan Sheehy was a rock star, as are her parents, Tim and Jean.

Tim says, "She was the focus of our hearts, our plans, and the life of our little family. We strove to give her the gifts of resilience, kindness, and a sense of wonder." Resilience, kindness, and a sense of wonder radiated from Megan, both before and after being diagnosed with osteosarcoma, an aggressive form of bone cancer, which took her life in 2014, two days after her fourteenth birthday.

Tim and Jean describe family life prior to her diagnosis: "Upon her return from school on Friday, a typical weekend started with her dropping her backpack on her shoes in the living room so she could greet Bella, our Westie. She often had plans with her friends from school, church, or the barn. Sleepovers were common, or we'd play a game or enjoy a movie together."

Megan spent Saturdays in their barn with her beloved pony, Missy B, and found tremendous confidence through her success as a competitive rider. Weekends that didn't involve horse shows were often filled with fun trail rides in the rolling woods and meadows of Essex County. She was at the barn three or four days a week for years and learned about responsibility by taking care of Missy B year-round.

"Sundays began at Old North Church in our home town of Marblehead. Megan had a pretty voice and sang in the children's choir for many years. During the summer, there were non-barn weekends aboard our sailboat, when we cruised with Megan to explore places from Maine to Connecticut. She was great about getting her homework done over the weekend, and she loved school. In fact, Megan always made time for her voracious reading habit on weekends. We happily avoided the middle school drama of Sunday evening stress about unfinished assignments."

The dichotomy of the life they were living versus the news they were about to receive created a unintentional change of cataclysmic proportion. Jean said, "At twelve years old, Megan found a new passion for volleyball. She played at school and begged us to enroll her in a clinic at a local college in the early summer. But she had pain in her lower leg, which we initially assumed was a combination of a new sport and the growing pains of a pre-teen."

Megan was not a complainer, so they saw her pediatrician when the pain didn't quickly recede. They eventually moved to a sports medicine specialist who happened to have done a rotation at Johns Hopkins that included rare pediatric sarcomas. He was suspicious of a subtle shadow on her fibula and biopsied it.

Tim remembers the day the doctors diagnosed her with cancer: "While awaiting results, we took off on our sailboat for Cape Cod to enjoy summertime in New England, which was a magical trip that included Megan's thirteenth birthday in Wellfleet. The next day, while sailing for Provincetown, we got the call from Mass General Hospital for Children's pediatric oncology group. They said that Megan had tested positive for osteosarcoma and needed to be seen as quickly as possible . . . A raging storm came through Provincetown the next day, with howling winds and driving rain from dark thunderclouds. In retrospect, it was pretty heavy-handed foreshadowing of the coming months."

In this book, we have talked about responding to change and have shared strategies to that end. Consider the Sheehys's description of how they responded: "No one ever wants that diagnosis, especially for their child. It was extremely serious and worrying. As a family of natural optimists with strong faith, an excellent community, and immediate access to Boston, which hosts several of the best hospitals in the world, we were certain that Megan would survive. We were equally certain that we were in for a life-defining challenge. We cried, we laughed, we shared our hopes and fears, and we began a deepening of our relationships that continues to be the most extraordinary of gifts."

Change ensued on a myriad of levels. First, there was the response to the diagnosis and then living with it. Her parents reflect, "In a word, Megan actively chose hope. With incredible strength and determination, she strove to live not as a victim, but as a survivor who was on a challenging path back to her normal life of school, friends, riding, and the wide-open possibilities of her future."

Certainly, someone in Megan's position could have chosen despair, but despair wasn't the route she chose. Tim describes his daughter's brave response: "Her hope was not denial of her cancer, which was an extremely rare and difficult type. She made us promise very early on that she would be involved in every decision, which we felt bound to honor. Megan had chosen the light and was fully open to seeing it in others. She became a favorite of the staff, from doctors, nurses, and child life staff to many of the unsung heroes, like personal care attendants, the housekeeping folks, and ultimately, the angels from hospice. While many admired her strength, it was her grace in being open, thankful, and authentic in her pursuit of a relationship with these people that made them love her. Megan would negotiate with her oncologist about treatment schedules around a concert or school dance. Because her doctor had a daughter the same age and because she deeply cared for Megan, she was incredibly accommodating within clinical limits."

According to Tim and Jean, this Mary Jean Irion poem encapsulates what Megan was working toward:

> Normal day, let me be aware of the treasure you are. Let me learn from you, love you, bless you before you depart. Let me not pass you by in quest of some rare and perfect tomorrow. Let me hold you while I may, for it may not always be so. One day I shall dig my nails into the earth, or bury my face in the pillow, or stretch myself taut, or raise my hands to the sky and want, more than all the world, your return.

Megan's parents are very clear that some days were a struggle, even with the hope she possessed and the effort she made to enjoy every day: "Megan's path had peaks and valleys. She kept her hope through chemo, which took her beautiful golden hair. We had a wig made of it for her, but she never wore it. 'This is who I am right now,' she said. 'People can just get over themselves about the hair.' It may have helped that she had the most remarkably perfect bald head! Just before Christmas, when the side effects of chemo were at a peak, leaving her sick and exhausted, she continued to be positive and wanted to celebrate the holidays at home as normally as possible. Even with the maximum doses of chemo that she could tolerate, the cancer came back and required amputating her leg above the knee."

Again, hope ruled Megan's response. "Megan chose to be charmed by her 'little leg,'" Tim and Jean share. They go on to say that the staff at the Massachusetts General Hospital were blown away by how quickly she was up and starting to learn mobility again. The nurses and child psychologist shared that many child amputees can't even bring themselves to look at their leg for a couple of days. Megan again chose a bold and hopeful path forward, despite the incredible challenges she faced, such as the "phantom" pain that affects so many new amputees.

The key for Megan was her choice to respond to this unintentional change with intention. While returning to school and beginning to master her new prosthetic, Megan rallied some friends and put on a musical benefit hosted at her charter school to raise money for an organization that funds art, music, computers, and entertainment supplies for Mass General's (MGH) pediatric floors. She raised an extraordinary amount of money and brought the community together in a spirit of gratitude to celebrate during a brief window of time when we were sure she was cancer free.

A number of her nurses and other MGH staff came to the weekend event. Tim recounts: "When one nurse was asked how many of such events she attended, she laughed and said, 'I've been in pediatrics for over twenty-five years, and this is a first.'" Tim and Jean make the point that Megan's hopefulness was contagious and had the effect of bringing out the best in people.

Sadly, Megan's remission would not last. She had her first scan three months after her amputation, and it left the Sheehys anxious. These trips were going to be part of their journey forward as a family and would always have some potential for bad news. "The scans were disastrous," Jean recalls. "The bone cancer had metastasized throughout her lungs and was clearly incurable. While there is always another possible chemo protocol, and these were offered, they were, by definition, longer shots."

Tim and Jean feel that the doctors at Mass General gave them an extraordinary gift that day. They suggested that as they considered the active medical options they also consider choosing to live life fully with the few months that Megan had left. As a family, they were unanimous in their choice of living life. They said, "As we spiraled our way up from the dark, lower levels of the Yawkey parking garage (another bit of heavy-handed metaphorical foreshadowing as we left the hospital behind), Megan, who was still thirteen, stated that she did not want to die in the hospital with IV-pump alarms and tubes and fluorescent lighting. She wanted to be at home in her own bed, with us there when her time came. We promised to make that happen."

Megan took seriously the charge of living each day to the fullest. Tim and Jean share this about her last months: "Generous friends made magical things happen, while being mindful of her capabilities. She'd said, for example, that she wanted to swim with dolphins. Some friends put together an amazing trip to Atlantis to grant that wish. While there, she climbed the Aztec temple on crutches to experience the waterslide through the Plexiglass tube running through a shark tank. It was such a blast she did it twice. "

That evening, while taking her around the quiet grounds in a wheelchair to see sawfish and other creatures in the exhibits, another mother approached us. She told us she'd seen Megan climbing that tower on crutches and was so inspired that she was recommitted to challenge her husband, who had a prosthetic foot and would never go out in public without it. She told Megan that her strength and openness were truly an inspiration. For the first time, Megan came to grips with the tension between just wanting to be a normal seventh-grader and people's constant comments that she was inspiring. Simply being Megan, with her strength and hope, was what people found inspiring."

She had a whiteboard on her bedroom wall with the activities planned for each coming day. Her range of activity contracted, first dropping plane trips, then longer car trips, and eventually even a visit to the barn became exhausting. Nonetheless, her friends and the community made possible whatever she could handle, right down to her last couple of days. She never failed to be thankful. With the astonishing assistance that is hospice, we were able to be Megan's parents, rather than exhausted primary caregivers, in her final days. We were at her bedside as a family when she passed."

It can be hard to know what to say or do in the face of tragedy. Sometimes the change we face is not ours, but that of those to whom we are connected. We were curious about the ways in which people were able to helpfully respond. The Sheehys explain what they found supportive: "People bring their gifts and skills forward to the edge of, and sometimes beyond, their comfort zone when presented with such an opportunity to live their values. People get it right when they offer comfort and help selflessly. When their gift was about Megan, and often, about the whole family, it was beautiful. This is love made visible. Megan's aunt, who is a clinical pharmacist in a hospital setting, was fantastic in growing her strong relationship with all three of us as a loving family member while also being invaluable in our decision making with the oncology team. Another close friend, with whose family we have vacationed, put her incredible organizational skills to work to ensure that offers of meals, rides, and other support flowed smoothly, while keeping Megan at the center of it all. Friends from the community and church who are cooks provided gourmet meals to our home. Others brought Megan appropriate gifts or simply made themselves available for a walk or a talk or a good cry."

They go on to share that their minister postponed a sabbatical he had earned after seven years of service simply to be available to them as time grew short. Friends with connections to cutting-edge, targeted-therapy biotech firms pushed their contacts to explore potentially appropriate experimental solutions. The Make-A-Wish Foundation bent over backwards to ensure she had an incredible experience, as Megan's initial choices were impossible. Her school counselor facilitated a circle of Megan's friends to be together in a safe way to share their deepest feelings with each other. We're talking about thirteen-year-old boys and girls putting themselves out there emotionally, completely vulnerable, in support of a friend they loved. Tim's colleagues, some of whom he had known for more than twenty-five years, selflessly covered his responsibilities so that he could be fully present. Tim and Jean agree that "it's the authenticity and selflessness of the offering that makes the gift perfect."

Unfortunately, some well-intended individuals might miss the mark. The potential of making matters worse is very real. As we share what the Sheehys have to say about this piece, we encourage you, our reader, to take their words to heart. Tim and Jean offer the following: "People would be well served to take a mindful look at the motivation driving them to a particular action. If it's being done out of obligation or any need of their own, it would be wise and compassionate to pause and examine that. In short, if it's about them at any level, rather than the family, it's probably not a good idea."

As parents of a terminally ill child, we were constantly pushing ourselves to do everything possible to love and comfort Megan. What is in shortest supply is time, and spare energy is close behind that. To try to exchange niceties over an impossible or inappropriate offer, however well intended, takes us away from what matters most. In a parallel vein, folks would do well, when sending cards or other messages, to carefully consider the words they are offering. In the case of terminal illness, suggestions that fighting hard enough or having deep enough faith will prevail simply aren't helpful. Cards and messages that beseech patients and parents, 'Don't give up!' are absurd. Giving up is not a consideration for the hopeful. Stopping a grieving parent who has barely summoned the will to go the grocery store with a stressfully earnest declaration of 'I don't know how you two do it!' just isn't helpful. [Rather, we would have appreciated if] they simply used Megan's name in a brief, authentic statement of their connection to her life or her example."

Both Tim and Jean are extraordinarily generous and candid in sharing. Nothing is off limits: "The process of parting with Megan's possessions has proven challenging, but sometimes rewarding. With help from her prosthetist, we were able to give her state-of-the-art prosthetic to a girl Megan's age who had come to the states with the support of a Boston Marathon bombing survivor for surgery following a horrific accident that took her leg. The giving served us as well as the gift has served her.

"Similarly, giving Megan's bike to a girl she used to babysit was soulful in the giving and receiving. Her favorite necklaces and other things have gone to cousins and friends. Many of her clothes and plush animals were donated to Syrian refugees through Marblehead's SPUR organization. We knew Megan would love that and happily volunteered to help sort the donations that filled two shipping containers.

"In all of these choices, we're simply trying to continue to learn and grow on our journey. No one chooses to walk the path of grieving parents, but we are on it for the rest of this life. The choice we do have is whether we can summon the grace to walk it in keeping with Megan's example of hope and strength."

The Sheehys have experienced the single most tragic kind of unintentional change—losing a beloved child. But her memory lives on: "We realize we continue to need stories of Megan. There are few more precious gifts than others sharing a story that we have not heard previously of Megan or her impact on their life. Similarly, pictures and especially videos are extraordinary, even if it's simply her goofing around with her BFFs on a random Saturday afternoon. We needed to learn what unconditional love is. Either of us would have willingly swapped places with Megan without a nanosecond's pause. There is no question that either of us would have taken on her suffering and given her back her future, without hesitation.

"We realized that we needed to revise our holiday traditions, because they could never be the same without Megan. We've volunteered on Christmas Day at Windrush Farm to feed and water the horses. Megan loved Windrush, and we're able to give members of the staff the holiday to be with their families. On Megan's birthday, we gathered her best friends and spent the morning harvesting and planting at the SPUR community garden. We delivered loads of fresh vegetables to the community food bank and planted a bunch of Megan's favorite flowers in a new garden to make the vegetable patch more beautiful. It was fantastic to honor Megan and be with her friends. I'm certain she was smiling on all of us."

It is a tremendous understatement to say the manner in which Megan and her family embraced this change is inspiring. They faced unintended change head-on, with respect, love, care, and a sense of urgency, accepting what they couldn't control and maximizing what they could. Megan was graceful, beautiful, and mature at the end of her life, which was no surprise to anyone around her. We can learn a lot from her about facing and conquering unintentional change. But maybe the most important lesson she leaves us with is that change is not a choice, but how you handle it is.

So how do we get out of winging it?

INTENTIONAL CHANGE

When life slaps us in the face with unintentional change, our response will determine our success in dealing with it. We may win a few battles if we choose to simply react to it in the moment, but the chances of winning the war are slim to none. Rather than flailing in the face of change, we need to meet uncertainty with deliberate intention.

As Brant illustrates, "Before becoming a musician, I spent half a decade in the commercial collections business, climbing the corporate ladder. Eventually, I became the vice president of business development. I was very good at my job, and the money was fantastic. But I felt this calling to pursue music ministry full-time. I laugh now that I had the audacity to try to 'make a deal' with God. If he would provide enough money for me to continue to live the lifestyle I lived, I would go out and sing for him.

"The problem with 'making a deal' with God is that you never know *how* he will answer. My company was acquired just six months after I made that deal. *We had a deal!* I was out of work for nine months. I made too much money for someone in his late twenties, and if I applied for something that paid less than I was making, my future employer would assume I would leave when something better came along. Oh, the joy of unintentional change.

"I knew I wanted to pursue music, but I needed a plan to make sure I achieved that goal. I moved my family back to New Hampshire and lived in my grandparents' house to save money until I finally accepted a job selling CAD/CAM software. I had no idea what I was selling, but I did know that this job would provide me the flexibility to do what was needed to execute my plan to play music. I set a date for six months in the future when I would quit that job and begin my music career. I spent that focused time diligently calling coffee shops, churches, and music venues at night, trying to book shows wherever I could.

"June 1, 2003, arrived, and as I looked at my calendar, something incredible stared back at me. I had booked seventy-five concerts over the next year. I exceed my goals, and I was finally ready to pursue my passion."

Intentional change requires a plan to follow. Vision, goal setting, clear metrics, and a powerful definition of success are all key elements to overcome the short-term challenges you'll face.

Whether it's committing to losing that "holiday weight" or embodying Gandhi's famous quote of "being the change you want to see in the world," intentional change begins with intention. You have crossed the bridge from "wanting" to "needing" change and are committed to bringing that change to fruition. Successfully engaging intentional change begins with the following:

1. **Having Vision:** As Stephen Covey famously instructed, we must "begin with the end in mind." However, we would add, beginning the end in mind does not provide details for the journey. Unless you possess a sixth sense or a crystal ball, vision is

essential. You must know what you want to accomplish and why. While the process of achievement is fluid and unique to the change-maker, you must have a clear vision for where you want to go and how you plan to get there.

2. **Setting Goals:** The answer to the age-old question, "How do you eat an elephant?" is simply, "One bite at a time." Goals must be clear, attainable, and portioned out in an achievable framework. We will talk more about this when we discuss success, but for now, see goal setting as determining the size of the bites you will take as you pursue your desired outcome.

3. **Establishing Clear Metrics:** Saying, "I want to make a bunch of money," or, "I want to lose a bunch of weight," is not as powerful as saying, "I want to earn one-hundred-thousand dollars," or, "I want to lose thirty-five pounds." By being clear in determining metrics, you will know when you are on or off track. Like goal setting, the road to ultimate success is lined with markers that indicate precisely how far you have come *and* how far you have to go.

4. **Defining Success:** The definitions of success are as varied as the personal missions they drive. Some involve luxurious material possessions, extraordinary power, or benevolent acts of human service. For some, it might be about the relationship they want or the achievements of their children. We are not concerned with any of those things. Instead, we define *success* as simply *making and keeping commitments.*

This is an important definition and a crucial point to consider. Defining success as "making and keeping commitments" allows you to repeatedly celebrate as you pursue whatever your ultimate desired change might be. Likewise, when commitments are broken, we can accept accountability and immediately get back on the horse and try again. If you want to lose thirty-five pounds, you might commit to working out three times a week. You'll be successful when you set a specific commitment and keep it. Stack one success on top of the other, and you will not only accomplish your goal but will also find tremendous satisfaction in the journey.

While these four points—casting and maintaining a vision, thoughtfully setting goals, establishing a measurable set of metrics, and adopting a sustainable definition of success—are incredibly important, meaningful, intentional change also requires us to connect to why it matters (determine our motivation) and to be honest about what it would cost the world or us if things just stay the same. The reason many find intentional change so challenging is that the things we feel "should" motivate us don't. We become stagnant in the absence of meaningful, individual motivation. The result? We wind up "should-ing" all over ourselves and never dig any deeper to determine what actually matters. Self-awareness and brutal honesty are critical to navigating the course and staying on track—even for those with the strongest of intentions. Without a clear connection to the "why," the "how" will be irrelevant.

Unintentional change is inevitable—like the kind that shows up on the last day of vacation or as bruises on your fourteen-year-old soccer player. The deep longings for impact and influence attached to intentional change are also, for many of us, part of the human experience. Both intentional and unintentional change are unavoidable and are also in fact interconnected as in many cases one gives rise to the other. When we attempt to make intentional change, the uncertainty of the outcome can lead to unintentional consequences.

When faced with change, it is also important to understand the difference between "reacting" and "responding." Reactivity elicits strong emotion that triggers our intrinsic fear, clouding our ability to effectively respond as we are dominated by our feelings. In contrast, when we are powerfully engaging with unintentional change, we can respond with thoughtful action, thus greatly increasing the likelihood of our desired result.

The next part of the book looks at how to craft your "set list" for dealing with change. This will combine several different strategies and serve as your plan to follow as you accomplish the change you seek. But before we can create that set list, we need to learn some songs (strategies).

LONG LIVE THE LP

LET'S TALK ABOUT JOURNEY (NOT THE BAND)

August 1, 1981, may not be a date that stands out in your mind, but this date is forever etched in history for any music lover. It was the birth of a cable television channel called MTV, which played music videos 24/7. Looking back, many of us take for granted what a revolutionary change this was to modern culture. Before MTV, if you wanted to see your favorite band, you bought a ticket and waited for them to come to a venue near you. All of that literally changed overnight.

The first music video ever played on the station, "Video Killed the Radio Star," was foreshadowing the effect this cable channel would have on the music world as a whole. It turned music into a multimedia experience. It filled in the gaps of our imagination, for better or worse. Iconic videos like Dire Straits's "Money for Nothing," and Michael Jackson's "Thriller," burned images into our brains that still exist almost forty years later. While MTV allowed us to see famous rock stars through the magic of music videos, the "album" was still the best way to dive into the hearts and minds of your favorite artist. Digging into the liner notes and reading the lyrics connected us to the soul of the album.

As Brant recalls, "I remember being nine years old, grabbing the album *Rock and Roll Over* by KISS, and sitting on the shag carpet in the living room, listening to the warm sound of vinyl. I would patiently wait for the songs 'Calling Dr. Love' and 'Hard Luck Woman' to play through my giant Pioneer headphones that took up half my face. Those songs were spread across the entire album, so I sat and listened to it in its entirety, rather than trying to drop the needle in the perfect spot to skip the songs I wasn't into. With time, I learned to love the songs in between. The album, taken as a whole, provided a deeper look into the artists' heart."

Those days are long gone.

While technology is, indeed, a wonderful thing, as we have learned, sometimes the unintentional causes incredible change. When we were kids, the Sony Walkman was the coolest of cool. We could take our tapes with us and listen to music with a small brick attached to our belt. As uncomfortable as it was, as much as its weight slowly pulled your pants toward the pavement, and even though it required you to carry a small piece of luggage to listen to more than one tape . . . everyone wanted one.

Fast forward a few decades, and my, oh, my, has technology improved. Apple creates the incomparable iPod. It is now possible to carry your entire music collection in your pocket. Leave the carry-on filled with tapes at home and forget about rewinding and fast-forwarding. Everything is now instantaneous and at the touch of a button. How awesome is that?! The intentional change that led to the innovation of the iPod had an incredible unintentional consequence: the impending death of the album—LP or long play, as we know it.

With the creation of iTunes, you could choose to buy *only* the song you liked, rather than purchasing the album to listen to the song you heard on the radio. This drove the music industry into a "singles-based" mentality, forcing artists to write songs they think a radio station will play, rather than writing music they love. Those constraints severely limited creativity. All of a sudden, the songs had to be less than four minutes, get to the chorus quickly, and play well to a general audience. Gone were the days where an album was a cohesive thought, telling a story throughout while allowing for the "deep cuts," the songs in the middle of the record, to find their way into people's hearts. The artist wants the deep cuts to be heard—as part of the story of his album— but they don't fit the format of what radio stations will play.

This development is right in line with the immediate-gratification culture in which we currently live. We unknowingly ask ourselves, "Why would I listen to a whole record when I can just listen to the one song I know I like?" Artists now have to try win over the audience in just one song, or listeners may never give their music another chance. Musicians no longer have the luxury of asking people to take the time to listen to an entire album. An album used to bring listeners on a nearly hour-long trip, climbing over mountains and dredging through valleys. Now, it's a race to the finish line.

You might be wondering, what does this have to do with change? Change isn't an all or nothing proposition. It's not a one-hit wonder. It's an epic journey filled with smash hits, tearful ballads, and some mundane filler in the middle. Taking the full journey of transformation—listening to the entire album, if you will—provides you with a memorable, impactful experience that provides context to the work at hand and allows the change to stick.

Don't get us wrong; we love the hits. Songs that stand out and reach the masses have reached us, too. In many ways, those are the songs that made us want to play music in the first place. Wanting to rock just like the artists we loved motivated us to pick up the guitar and practice. Molly Fletcher is one of those artists in the leadership world. Through our interview with her, we learned some valuable lessons about how true rock stars navigate real change.

ROCK STARS OF CHANGE: MOLLY FLETCHER

Molly Fletcher is a trailblazer in every sense of the word—a rare talent of business wisdom, relationship brilliance, and unwavering optimism. As a CEO and successful entrepreneur, she shares her unconventional and unique techniques that made her one of the first female sports agents in the high-stakes, big-ego world of professional sports. Formerly, as president of client representation for sports and entertainment agency CSE, Molly spent two decades as one of the world's only female sports agents. She was hailed as the "female Jerry Maguire" by CNN as she recruited and represented hundreds of biggest names in sports, including Hall of Fame pitcher John Smoltz, PGA TOUR golfer Matt Kuchar, broadcaster Erin Andrews, and basketball championship coaches Tom Izzo and Doc Rivers. As she successfully negotiated over five hundred million dollars in contracts and built lasting relationships, she also observed and adopted the traits of those at the top of their game.

In our interview, we ask Molly, "What was the hardest change you've ever faced in your life?" She offers a compelling response: "The hardest change I've ever faced in my life . . . well, what comes up to me first is that in general I didn't tell myself changes were hard, so I never believed that they were hard. But beyond that, I can tell you about the two biggest changes in my life. The first was leaving my hometown and moving away from my two incredible parents and a close family.

"Most folks thought I'd stay in Michigan because my family and I were so close – and we still are. But I think subconsciously I needed to go do my own thing. I needed to go out, see what I was made of. Yes, it would be hard to move to Atlanta with only a small amount in savings. But I was young and I never thought it was hard, so it was never hard.

"I think it's so much of what we tell ourselves. Looking back, yes, it was hard. But I didn't over think it. I didn't think, 'OK if this move works that means I'm going to work in Atlanta, get married here, have kids here, and this will be my home.' That didn't go through my head. I just knew I wanted to go out on my own, so I did what I needed to do.

"The second biggest change in my life was leaving a job with a salary more than I ever thought I'd make in my life, with a boss that I really appreciated. My boss and I had a wonderful friendship. That was hard, because I left with only nine speaking engagements on my calendar that totaled five percent of my annual salary.

"But I just knew that I could be successful, whether it was my speaking or something else in the sports industry. I always believed that it would work, and I think when we tell ourselves that, it does become a reality.

"For example when my daughter goes to play a tennis match, and she's going out to play the first seed, and she says, 'Mom, this first seed is going to be really hard.' I remind her 'No, you've got this. It's only hard if you tell yourself it's hard. And, PS we can do "hard" '"
Hearing her response, we ask, "How did you sort of work yourself through the changes you were experiencing?"

"I grew up in an environment with an enormous amount of common sense, hard work, and a Midwest value system. It was one of those things where I knew that if I just kept moving the ball down the field, I'd score. Yes, I was on the ten-yard line (with 90 years to go)… if I worked hard, the next day it'd be fourth and ten again, and then I'd get going, and I'd keep going, and I'd keep going.

"I talked about that in my book Fearless at Work: it's little moments, yet big outcomes. I believe that if you're working harder and smarter then you did the next day before…if you are you're grinding and getting after it, you can't help but win somehow, some way. I would say that was probably the biggest thing; I believe that kind of grind--it mindset leads to positive results."

Her response leads us to think about the relationship between change and consequences: "When you made these changes, what were the unintentional consequences that came about?"

"It's one thing to have a nice lifestyle business that has high margins and nice cash flow, and then it's another thing to make it a company that's beyond yourself. That's harder but it's possible. It's what I am working on now, all the stuff that happens behind the scenes. What I've learned is I'm not an operator, so I've put people around me that are. I'm more of a visionary and have an entrepreneurial mindset, so it's important for me to have people around me that are different from me. It allows us to come together with our different strengths and be even better.

"That was something I didn't know when I left my job as a sports agent. I'd say one of my assets is I like to listen to a lot of advice; I like to ask people a lot of questions. But it is also a liability because I get a lot of information from a lot of different people, which sometimes can be confusing.   For example, people ask, 'Why do you always talk about your athletes? Why don't you talk about yourself?' But my initial response was that people would rather hear about John Smoltz, Doc Rivers and Tom Izzo rather than me. I'd think to myself, 'Why would they want to hear my story?' But eventually I was persuaded that people wanted to hear my stories too, so that was when I decided to give it a try.

"So in speeches I started to weave in some of my personal stories, and afterwards people would comment, 'You know that story about your twins? That was so cool. Thank you for sharing that,' or, 'That story about your moving to Atlanta, I really connected with it.' The feedback was telling me that I needed to tell these stories.' One consultant we hired asked, 'Why are you so private?' I responded that I wasn't private. She stood her ground, and I simply let her know that maybe it was because no one had ever told me that. I started thinking on it, and I realized I didn't talk about myself much because I hadn't accomplished as much as the guys that I represented, so people all day long would rather hear about them than me."

Molly reinforces the notion that you have to fold your own narrative into the process of change. Change is unique to every person in this world and doesn't mean the same thing to each and every one of us. So, we ask Molly: "Was there a compelling event or reason that you decided you wanted to go your own way and do your own thing?"

"Yes, definitely. Morgan Stanley came to me after my speaking got going a little bit. And said, 'Look, we want you to do all of our new hires, and we want you to do all of our transitional hires, and we want you to do all of our zero- to three-year service hires,' but I said, 'Wait — I've got fifteen keynotes on the book.'

"Fast forward to when I was on an airplane on my way home from a speech. I was still full-time as an agent and had a team of agents, and we represented about three hundred athletes. I got off the airplane and a couple of my athletes had tried to call me on the plane but they went my voicemail since I couldn't answer. The truth was, I was so connected to my guys that they really didn't go to voicemail much. It sort of made my heart sink because I thought, 'Man, I am having a bandwidth problem here. I can't do both of these things, and I'm going to need to make a decision.'

I remember a conversation with John Smoltz when he asked, 'What are you doing? Where are you? Who are you going to see in New York? What were you doing in there? Were you going to see so-and-so player?' I told him 'No, I was giving a speech.' He asked what I meant and what I was speaking about. It was like my job was to represent him, not me, and now I was sort of representing me.

"It hit me then that I couldn't authentically do both any more. I couldn't let my players go to. And I wasn't going to be able to be as present as I needed to be at the agency if I was doing fifteen days of speeches. And the speaking engagements were sort of just coming in off referrals. So that was one moment, and then the other moment was after a speech when someone said, 'Thank you. You need to keep doing this. The world needs this.' And the truth was, I never had an athlete ever say, 'Keep being my agent. You are changing my life.'

"I just thought that I had a little bit of a calling, if you will, or a gift here that I need to do.' So, there were those two moments that made me think I needed to do this.

"Then my husband and I sat down and really talked through it, and thankfully he was remarkably supportive and said, 'Go for it.' The truth is, I wish I had made the change sooner. Oftentimes after people make a change, they just think 'Man, why didn't I do this earlier?'"

Molly's comments remind us that meaningful, intentional change requires us to connect to our inner stirrings. You must respond to the change slowly infiltrating your life and ask yourself if it matters and why it matters (determine your motivation). Then, be honest about what it would cost you (or even the world) if you resist the change and keep things the same. Real change requires commitment and vision.

ROCK 'N' ROLL SECRET: THE FIRST SONG ALMOST ALL GUITARISTS OVER THE AGE OF THIRTY LEARNED TO PLAY IS THE ROCK CLASSIC "SMOKE ON THE WATER" BY DEEP PURPLE. IT IS A RITE OF PASSAGE. WHAT IS THE FIRST SONG GUITARISTS UNDER THE AGE OF THIRTY LEARNED TO PLAY? TRICK QUESTION . . . GUITAR HERO DOES NOT ACTUALLY EVEN INVOLVE A GUITAR. *KIDDING!* NOT KIDDING.

GET UP OFFA THAT THING

How many times have you either said or heard someone else say, "I know what to do, but I don't do it." She'll usually offer this statement with a tone of either frustration or resignation. A frustrated person seems tortured by a perceived inability to change. She is puzzled about why she is still stuck in a feeling, behavior, job, body, relationship, or situation that is unsatisfying at best and destructive at worst. A resigned person is past that point and has given up. She claims to have done her best and has decided to accept her plight. Even though she knows what to do, she sees herself as incapable of actually doing it.

Wherever we may fall between frustration and resignation, being honest about the possibility that we may not really want to change will save us a lot of time and energy. Let us say this again: some of us may not want to change. Getting real about not wanting to change frees us up to discover what we actually *do* want. The whole frustrated/resigned thing may in fact just be a pose that communicates to the world, "I know I'm supposed to want this." However, being able to openly say, "I know I'm supposed to want this, but I don't," is a gift, not only to ourselves but also to the people who are invested in us.

One of the most important things we can do is to encourage you to unburden yourself. That, in and of itself, may be the most powerful personal change you experience from reading *Rock 'n' Roll with It*. With all of that in mind, if you are still stuck, moving forward may require you to identify what *actually* motivates you.

You must understand, what motivates others may not motivate you. So, when it comes to motivation for change, many of us live trapped within cultural norms that are not working. For example, maybe you want to quit smoking. In response, people have asked, "Don't you want to live long enough to play with your grandkids?" We know they are trying to help, and we feel as if we should be motivated by this goal, but it doesn't meaningfully motivate us to change. Thus, unknowingly, we allow shame to enter the picture. Any efforts then end. We think or say things like, "Well if *that* didn't motivate me to change, nothing will!" But, motivation is not one size fits all. It requires custom tailoring and a committed search for the perfect fit, and that quest is primarily internal. With this in mind, look inside and discover your personal motivation.

Many of us are a lot like Mick Jagger: we try and we try and we try and we try, but we "can't get no satisfaction." At the core of our personal motivation is a tug-of-war between satisfaction and dissatisfaction. When satisfaction is winning the match, our motivation to pull harder just isn't there. When dissatisfaction finds itself in the driver's seat, not only will we dig deeper to find the motivation needed to win, we may hear of a "supernatural" strength that is mysteriously found.

In fact, the desire for change is often born out of some form of dissatisfaction or deprivation. Deprivation and dissatisfaction inspire us to search for solutions and take action in service of our goals. The level of dissatisfaction one can tolerate ultimately comes down to the individual. Some have it carved into their minds that they need to hit rock bottom first. This notion is not only untrue but also wastes time and does unnecessary damage. If you have been waiting to hit rock bottom, *raise the floor.*

Discovering our personal motivation begins by identifying what we feel deprived of. Then, we can determine what's causing the deprivation. We'll provide tools for actively engaging this process later in the book, but for now, a quick survey of what you're hungry for and why may bring up some potential solutions.

You could love your job but still be a little stressed and overworked. Being deprived of downtime inspires you to take a vacation. A couple of satisfying weeks on the beach with an umbrella drink in your hand fills you up and magically you're ready to head back to the cubicle. Or perhaps you don't love your job and haven't for a very long time. Your boss is cruel, your co-workers are beaten down, and you find the work meaningless. You are deprived of respect, encouragement, and a sense of purpose. You are dissatisfied with how your colleagues are treated. The actions required to address the situation might seem overwhelming, but examining the details of what you are actually deprived of will not only help you to strategize a long-term solution, but it may also bring temporary relief as well.

Science demonstrates that consequences shape our behavior. Our level of motivation (which is determined by our level of deprivation) establishes the value and degree of influence those consequences have on our actions. In radical behavior analysis, a discipline with broad application, it's considered a best practice to assess which motivations and outcomes likely maintain behavior, before trying to change it. Working with Susan Shea, ED. S., we developed a memorable way to help determine your motivation. Thanks to Sir Isaac Newton's bold imagination that led him to measure the color spectrum with musical scales, an iconic image of a prism is permanently etched in our psyche, as well as on Pink Floyd's hugely successful album "Dark Side of the Moon." Given its familiarity and association to music, PRISM, is an acronym well suited for classifying motivation into five specific areas:

PERCEPTUAL, REMOVAL, INTERPERSONAL, SENSATIONAL AND MATERIAL.

PERCEPTUAL: This category isn't an underlying motivation, but a factor that can pervasively influence all motivation, for good or for bad. Our perception of possible consequences influences our actions as much as the consequences we experience. Perceived consequences come from our vast history of learning and observing others. We can be well informed or misinformed by our perceptions, so it's important to be aware of them. Once identified, we can put their veracity to the test. Some questions we can ask in order to examine certain perceptions include: "Is this really true?," "Is this the only truth?," and "What other outcomes haven't I considered?" Conclusions we draw about potential consequences have a strong influence on the actions we do or do not take.

REMOVAL: Behavior can be motivated by our desire to avoid aversive experiences (e.g., pain, discomfort, loss, demands) or by a lack of reinforcement. Many creative solutions and ingenious inventions were born out of our motivation to remove something aversive, like finding a cure for an illness. Hence the proverb, "Necessity is the mother of invention." Motivation to avoid can also occur when we have an insufficient history of reinforcement for doing something. Unless you're someone who loves the thrill of the unknown, you may feel apprehensive or unmotivated when called to act. Due to an insufficient history of reinforcement, a child complains about going to his piano lesson. He's motivated to remove the experience because of a lack of reinforcement.

He goes to the piano lesson any way, motivated again by removal, but of a different sort—namely the wrath of his mother. We may not feel motivated to act until we engage in a behavior for a sufficient time to allow reinforcement to follow. With this awareness, you may be able to give yourself the extra push you need to begin something you've been putting off due to temporary discomfort you may experience.

INTERPERSONAL: From the moment we were born, social consequences have been shaped and maintained our actions in powerful ways. Even seemingly benign, inadvertent attention and behavior of others affect how we live. Our parents or parental figures largely shaped our values and therefore our actions. To help identify interpersonal motivations, we can ask ourselves: "Whom am I doing this for?," "Do I want (person's) needs or expectations to influence my decision?," "Who do I respect and admire?," "and "What would they do in a similar circumstance?" We aren't exactly free to choose how others influence us, but we are free to choose our relationships, values, role models and mentors. In considering the influence that interpersonal relationships have on our actions, we may be empowered by looking at our internal relationships as well. We have a unique ability as humans to observe our inner world. We're made up of a myriad of talents, tendencies and rebels that have continuous dialogue and sometimes experience conflict. Ultimately, if we establish our role as a non-judgmental observer of these inner parts, we can unify these aspects of ourselves. Our relationship with our self may be the most transformative relationship we can have.

SENSATIONAL: This category has to do with our primal urges (e.g., sexual desire, hunger, thirst, fatigue) and sensory experiences (e.g., olfactory, taste, auditory, visual, tactile.) When someone is motivated to play a musical instrument without an audience, her personal sensory experience is what motivates her. Our sensational motivation is so basic; it's easy to think it doesn't influence us much. However, if sufficiently deprived, this type of motivation can completely control our behavior. For example, if someone neglects his need for sleep, then his motivation for sleep can take over. For our purposes, it's important to be aware that this type of motivation is in play all the time.

MATERIAL: Material motivation involves a desire for things or activities that we seek to do or acquire, that are not interpersonal or sensational. This might include money, food, clothing, vehicles, medicine, housing, etc....This is an important motivation often linked to survival instincts. Even an altruistic person's behavior can be influenced by competing motivation for material reinforcement. For example, a nurse who wants to help others because of the interpersonal reinforcement may still leave the job if the pay is too low. This would be material motivated action.

When considering your underlying motivations, it's important to know that we tend to have multiple motivations at once that can compete with each other. This is usually what's happening when we have difficulty making a decision about what action we should take. While you contemplate your motivations, be curious. Observe yourself nonjudgmentally and keep your sense of humor. We humans are wired to be lazy, impatient, pleasure-seeking, pain-avoidant animals. But even though that's how our engine runs, steering the rig is in our hands.

Ultimately, we find that motivation is about the deep longings of our hearts and minds and our level of satisfaction or deprivation in a particular area. Your desire for change hums constantly in the background. Will you be able to look over your life from a rocking chair in a nursing home and be okay with what you did or did not accomplish? Will you take your final breath and be okay with not starting that company, pursuing that passion, overcoming that heartache, or making that change? Brutal honesty and self-awareness will be critical to staying on track.

CREATING YOUR SET LIST

Just as an artist writes an entire album to take the listener on a journey, he repeats the same process when creating a set list for his live concerts—the whole undertaking is a science, really. He carefully plans "moments" and "experiences" throughout his ninety-minute performance, hoping to engage the audience and provide a memorable experience.

World-renowned live music producer Tom Jackson has been teaching artists how to create "moments" within a performance for decades. He has worked with some of the biggest acts in music, including Taylor Swift and The Band Perry. Jackson believes that a well-constructed set list can create an emotional connection with the audience powerful enough to change their lives.

He says, "Now, success means different things to different people. It may mean making and recording your own music or being able to play your music regularly in your area to fans who love you . . . But where that success you dream of will ultimately come from is your live show."

We are going to use the analogy of creating a set list to construct a finely tuned plan to successfully bring about the transformational change we now seek. Whether you are facing intentional or unintentional change, we are going to equip you with three strategies to use when approaching either. These strategies are designed to be used together in a "set list" and to match the level of commitment you are willing to give in the moment. A well-thought-out set list includes three types of songs:

Cover Songs: Every musician learns her craft by playing someone else's song. Playing a "cover song" is like using a roadmap; the chords and lyrics have already been written, and the melody is established. The pressure is minimal because you don't have to start from scratch. Thus, the Cover Song Approach for change is low risk and produces a reliable reward. The ease of following a pre-constructed plan makes it an effective first step.

Sampled Songs: The process of taking a familiar piece of a cover song and using it to create another song is called *sampling*. When a musician has mastered a cover, he can then alter it in a way that makes it his own. When we use the Sampled Song Strategy to approach change, we rely on the familiar part of a cover song to serve as a comfortable foundation on which to build. By adding our contribution to the mix, we raise the risk and accountability slightly, but we also hope to increase the impact.

Original Songs: Taking an idea, a melody, and a lyric you have thought of and combining them together to create something completely unique is the process of writing an original song. It allows you to express yourself in a way only you can. The Original Song Strategy to change requires vulnerability as you engage your Own Original Voice (OOV). This strategy is high risk as the accountability rests squarely on your shoulders. However, the results are the most impressive and have the highest impact on us personally.

An artist will use all three of these types of songs to effectively engage an audience. Each serves a specific purpose in connecting to even the most hardened hearts of fans. When and where we use these songs within a performance depends on a number of factors. Over the next few chapters, we will dissect each strategy and learn when and how to effectively use it when faced with change in our own lives.

THE "SHO" SHIN MUST GO ON: THE COVER SONG APPROACH

CHANGE STARTS HERE

A "cover" is a song we play that was made famous by someone else. It takes lots of hard work—and maybe even a little bit of luck—to play a song exactly like Eddie Van Halen does. Singing like Alicia Keys is no easy feat, either, yet people all over the world are practicing right now to do just that. The reasons these would-be artists give it a shot are as diverse as the styles of music they are trying to copy. Some have stars in their eyes and long for fame. Others are looking for a hobby, wanting a new skill set, or trying to impress a girl.

While playing music is satisfying, expressive, and fun, it is also really hard—especially when you are just starting out. Anyone who has taken a guitar lesson knows your fingertips pay a price when pushing strings down over and over again until you can play the song cleanly and as written. We push through the discomfort until calluses form, making a sore hand from trying to play the chords nothing more than a work hazard. That unavoidable pain causes many to quit before they even really get started and leads to an unwillingness to practice.

As Brant tells it, "I started playing guitar when I was twelve years old. My parents had signed me up for lessons at Ted Herbert's Music Mart in downtown Manchester, New Hampshire. My guitar teacher, Jerry, was an accomplished jazz musician. His ability to play crazy difficult chords and make it look effortless was both awe inspiring and frustrating. I was trying to learn to play "I Wanna Rock and Roll All Night" by KISS and was having some trouble getting my fingers to cooperate.

"Jerry wanted me to learn some other music that focused more on technique and theory. My fingertips were so bruised from practicing that every time I went to play a note, I would wince. My left hand was cramping from all the abnormal stretching the chords required. I couldn't take it. I stopped practicing. I would show up every week for my lesson and play the same song poorly and without improvement. Jerry was frustrated, I was defeated, and I eventually told my parents I didn't want to play anymore."

One of the central tools for becoming a proficient musician is learning to play covers. For many, that's where it all begins, and it is part of the process to accept that learning these first songs can be uncomfortable and occasionally painful. The challenge is to stick with it and play through the temporary torment. Remember, a real rock star takes risks and has enough swagger to carry him through difficult times.

Copying is easier than creating. When copying, a talented musician who came before you already determined the chords and the melody, leaving you only to memorize the lyrics. Like a paint by number, knowing what the song is supposed to sound and feel like provides a clear template; you can tell when you are getting it right.

When working toward change, think of learning or playing cover songs as a metaphorical approach. This approach is perfect when you are hungry for change but don't have the foggiest idea how to do it. Many times, we have the desire to change but lack the initiative to "create" it. The Cover Song Approach allows us to begin on a path toward change by simply following pre-written instructions.

Losing weight is a great example of where the Cover Song Approach to change works like a charm. For many people, it is a mystery what healthy, balanced eating really looks like. Therefore, countless programs were created to tell participants exactly what to eat and when. For people who may have played around at losing weight on their own and failed, a pre-programmed Cover Song Approach, when adhered to, can be incredibly effective at producing results.

We once sat next to a woman in a diner who could have really used this book. She ordered the double cheeseburger club, medium rare. However, she wanted the fries well done (Jim adds that this is an advanced move) and a large Dr. Pepper. Her tone of voice changed with her next request. Slowly and deliberately, she told the waitress that it was imperative that her sandwich be served on whole wheat bread. She slowly repeated those words, as if to emphasize them. She went on to explain that she had put herself on a *very* strict diet and that she would have to send her meal back if the bread was wrong. The Cover Song Approach would have sent her straight to Genevieve Guidroz, whom you will recognize by her stage name, Jenny Craig.

When Genevieve opened her first weight loss center in Australia, over thirty years ago, she never could have imagined that all these years later she would have centers around the world and three-thousand employees. She also wasn't thinking about cover songs, but she was unknowingly writing a song that would be covered by millions.

The company motto is, "With Jenny Craig, you don't have to count, track, or worry about what to eat. We give you everything you need to succeed!" Participants sign up and are told or sold exactly what to eat and drink and when. Jenny takes the guesswork out of exercise as well. The song is already written. Every lyric, beat, chorus, and frozen lasagna is provided to the consumer—no creativity required and no need to question whether you are singing in tune. Jenny's goal is that eventually you will learn from this process and move on to what we are going to address in the next chapter (sampled songs). For now, we just want you to consider the power and simplicity of using the Cover Song Approach to engage your mission.

When it comes to creating change, the Cover Song Approach allows us to know when we are getting things right and to sense when we're aren't. The benefit of having instructions to refer back to is that we don't veer too far from the writer or creator's design. With the ability to see what something "should" look like, the probability of making mistakes decreases as we have a pattern before us. The accountability increases as the rules, protocols, and boundaries are clearly indicated up front. Either you have followed the instructions, or you haven't.

For some of us, if at first we don't succeed, that's all it takes to make us stop. However, the idea of "try, try again" can't be a deal breaker for any serious change-maker. Whether learning a cover or creating change, the number of times we might need to try, try again can be discouraging and requires not only resilience and commitment but also humility.

Shoshin is a Japanese word that is literally translated as "first visit." But, when applied to Zen Buddhism, it is understood to mean "beginner's mind." Achieving beginner's mind requires an enthusiasm for learning and an openness to the process. Shoshin frees the student from the notion that she is supposed to be able to skip steps, jump ahead, or just intrinsically know how to do something without being taught.

The woman at the diner, who was convinced that whole wheat bread was going to make her lose weight, might wonder where the mysterious pounds she's continuing to gain are coming from. What she would learn in just one session at Jenny Craig would likely blow her away and change her eating habits, yet her arrogance, pride, and ignorance are the enemies of a beginner's mind and are, interestingly, often fueled more by insecurity than confidence. These attributes are paralyzing at best and embarrassing at worst. We need to be willing to begin as beginners when following a Cover Song Approach to change. Only then can we wholeheartedly embrace the process of learning and advancement.

Starting something new, as we mentioned earlier, can be downright painful. The wise beginner is aware of this and accepts the initial discomfort as part of the process. He also knows practice is the key to moving beyond the pain. Practice, contrary to popular opinion, does not make perfect. Perfection, as it relates to human endeavors, does not exist. Even after a couple weeks at Jenny Craig, our friend from the diner will slip up. Well-done fries are crispy, delicious, and they whisper lies. A trip through the Wendy's drive through might be her version of hitting a wrong note. It's part of the journey.

Rarely do we hear someone say, "It came out so great because I'm a perfectionist." The term *perfectionist* is usually used as part of an excuse as to why someone didn't get something done in time or didn't even start. Practice makes a lot of things, but perfect is not one of them. What practice does do, apart from getting us through the initial discomfort of change, is make us proficient, accomplished, steadfast, and productive. As we discussed in chapter 4, success is simply *making and keeping commitments.* When we commit to practice, each session is a success unto itself. As famed composer Ignacy Jan Paderewski once said, "If I miss one day of practice, I notice it. If I miss two days, the critics notice it. If I miss three days, the audience notices it."

Typing the word *fail* into YouTube yields over seventy-seven million videos: ice skaters falling, yoga moves turning into accidental gymnastics, skateboarders incurring catastrophic injuries, and American Idol auditioners making complete and utter "asses" of themselves. You're never gonna see us publically in a downward dog, but we can both tell horror stories of times when we crashed and burned during a live performance. While anyone who regularly performs is going to experience awkward/embarrassing moments, our job is to make sure we have done everything in our power to ensure that doesn't happen. Our stage is set smack dab between half-baked and perfectionism. The key here is to ensure that whatever you are presenting or the change you are working toward is ready for the world.

As you work toward mastery, you will need a trusted opinion. As hard as this is to hear, your family and friends will most likely not be objectively honest with you. Furthermore, they will usually work to convince you that they *are* being honest. When it comes to mastering a cover song, you need a qualified voice teacher. This is someone who has worked hard to become an expert and, therefore, has expert advice to offer. She is skilled and objective and knows students will tell others they studied with her. Her name and reputation are on the line, so she will give you honest feedback and helpful suggestions to get better.

Using the Cover Song Approach to change is no different. By engaging the opinions of experts, we are able to confirm that we are on the right track and ready to move forward. But submitting ourselves to such scrutiny requires a thick skin. If your mom tells you how beautiful you sing but your voice teacher kindly lets you know that you have a long way to go, it may feel like a shocking disappointment. The Cover Song Approach to change requires outside, objective, experienced input. It also requires us to put on our big-boy panties and keep working when we don't hear what we want to hear.

ROCK STARS OF CHANGE: ANDREW AND RYAN BELTRAN

When brothers Andrew and Ryan Beltran decided they wanted to "start a brand" in 2012, they weren't exactly in a position to make that happen. Andrew was completing his service in the Marines, and Ryan was a part-time English teacher in Guangzhou, China. They saw an opportunity to create something new in the wristwatch community. Original Grain is now the premier manufacturer of all-natural wood and steel watches. Several successful crowd-funding campaigns later, what started as simply an interesting idea has blossomed into a thirty-million-dollar business.

Converting an idea into a real, functioning business has many challenges. Partnering with a steel manufacturer and a woodcutting source to provide all the pieces necessary to produce a quality product was difficult to near impossible. Deciding when to change partners and what processes to bring in-house has also been a learning experience for the brothers. With Andrew investing nearly ten thousand dollars of the money he earned serving in the military to get production started, it's hard not to place an enormous focus solely on the revenue.

As Andrew tells us, "One of the biggest changes for me personally was developing and committing to a business plan, rather than stressing over everyday revenue. Starting a business is a process, and as a small team, things don't turn overnight. We had to commit ourselves to what we identified as best practices for our product line." It turned out to be a product line that saw a sudden, huge increase in demand after launching their first Kickstarter campaign in 2013. Crushing their initial goal of ten-thousand dollars, Original Grain raised nearly four-hundred-thousand dollars from over two-thousand individual backers. That type of demand forced these young entrepreneurs to face some incredible unintentional change. While they were prepared for meeting their goal, the overwhelming success presented some real, unexpected challenges.

Andrew remembers back to these early days and how they had to switch suppliers four times to get the quality and production times for which they were looking. He describes the experience: "As a start-up and new to business, there was always unexpected things that came up. New findings or channels we found success in, we would need to provide more resource to those areas."

Having a sudden demand for their product, they found themselves trying to battle the "low man on the totem pole" reality with their manufacturers. Being a small, boutique watchmaker producing a few hundred watches was very different than producing the thousands that were needed to meet demand. Andrew and Ryan had to plan some intentional change to ensure their product would end up in the hands of their crowd-funding backers.

They changed the qualifying questions they were asking to find what they were looking for. They researched who the manufacturers were working with to ensure they had the experience needed to produce the unique-quality product they wanted. Producing something completely original presented unintentional change to the manufacturers vying for their business. They had to look at the current processes and make adjustments to marry wood and steel.

Being original is comfortable for Andrew. He has held that desire for as long as he can remember. He developed his OOV when he was only a teenager: "My OOV is something that I feel has always been inside of me since I was young—fifteen to sixteen years old. Coming from a small town, this would get me in trouble from time to time. I didn't like following corporate structure and doing things the same as everyone. Being unique and original is engrained in my DNA. I don't need to be the center of attention, by any means, but I'll be in the corner doing my own thing. With our watch company, we designed something that was not on the market."

The brothers could have only taken the Cover Song Approach to making watches. Watches have been produced for centuries. They could have just decided to follow the process already created. Instead, they added their Own Original Voice to the watchmaking world and came up with new processes and designs to support making their wood and steel watches.

Curious about the tipping point for Andrew and Ryan, we ask if there was a moment of clarity that inspired the Original Grain brand.

Andrew explains, "Many acts of fate helped create our brand. While returning home from deployment, we had three days R&R in Hong Kong. Ryan was there teaching English at the time. I told him we were stopping so he could make sure to be available those few days. When I got there, we drank many beers, and he gave me my first watch ever. This watch reminded me instantly of our home in Oregon. After being gone for so long and being in my mindset, it was an instant relief every time I looked down at that watch. He told me he found this at a manufacturer and we could design these to be way cooler and incorporate the wood grain and steel look we wanted. He just needed some cash.

"Coming back from deployment, I gave him everything I saved so we could start this company and pursue a dream of working together in California . . . Five years later, we're trending toward thirty-million dollars and not looking back!"

Now that is some serious change! But even then, that might sound like a long shot to you. Don't worry. We will help you get there. To help you get started, let's take a look at a few techniques or nailing the Cover Song Approach.

CHOOSE THE RIGHT COVER SONG

Songs carry power. In fact, they can serve as literal time machines. In a few bars, we can be transported back to our first dance. Or we hear the tune our mom sang to us when she tucked us in, and we are carried back to childhood. Or we hear the song played at the funeral service for our grandfather, and we grow melancholy. Songs associated with memories can instantly transport us to far away times and places.

Bob Dylan talks about his early songs with wonder, unsure of how he wrote them. As songwriters, we revel in the moments when a song shows up in our hearts and makes its way onto the stage. Tapping into that seemingly magical power is one of the keys to being inspired enough to keep practicing. A love for music and the desire to perform ultimately elicits an emotional response as we recognize the beauty and power intrinsic to this pursuit.

Our passionate response to music in general and certain songs in particular propels us forward, and our experience leads us to one truth: if we are going to learn to play a cover, it's imperative that we choose the right song. If you have ever watched any of the singing competition shows, you know that choosing the right song for an audition can be the difference between success and failure. We have all flipped through the laminated three-ring binder on karaoke night looking for the perfect song to sing.

With regard to change, the first barrier to entry is choosing a "cover" that we actually like. It may sound obvious, but you'll never want to perform a cover of something you don't personally appreciate. Without love for the song, why would you put in the time to practice? Therefore, we need to hold a meaningful connection to the metaphorical song we choose.

Another important factor in choosing our "cover" is finding a song that will imbue us with the confidence needed to perform it well. The wrong song will frustrate, confound, and shine a light on what we can't and shouldn't do as a beginner. Frustration can lead us down a path of excuses. Therefore, the song we choose should be one that we can actually envision ourselves mastering in a reasonable about of time.

THE RIGHT SONG CHOICE SYNCHRONIZES OUR HEARTS, MINDS, WORDS, AND ACTIONS INTO A POWERFUL SYMPHONY OF PERSONAL GROWTH AND EXPANSION.

And, on the other end of the spectrum, don't pick a song beneath your skill level. Cover songs that are too easy don't help us grow. Keep in mind that playing our chosen cover well *should* take a bit of hard work. Being a little intimidated—yet not overwhelmed—by the effort needed is a good indicator that you've made the right choice. You won't be a beginner forever.

PERFORM YOUR COVER SONG AS IF YOU WROTE IT

You will eventually want to perform the cover as though you wrote it yourself. Frank Sinatra did not write "My Way." The Beatles did not write "Twist and Shout," and Jimi Hendrix did not write "All along the Watchtower." Shocked? Many of our favorite songs performed by our favorite artists were in fact cover songs. It's hard to imagine anyone other than Sinead O'Connor singing "Nothing Compares to You." The iconic music video of a simple yet powerful close-up shot of her face as she performs the song is legendary. She embodied every breath of those words—to tears—but she didn't actually write the song. It was written by the Purple One himself, Prince. The song resonated so deeply with Sinead that each performance was given as if she labored over the lyrics and melody herself.

We talked about choosing the right cover song, and those iconic covers could not have been better chosen; however, choosing well is not enough. When we choose the Cover Song Approach for change, we need to own it. Owning it means becoming so intimately connected to the prescribed process that it feels like it's part of us. We must enthusiastically embrace all the complexities and nuances through memorization, which leads to internalization and, ultimately, to application. The goal is to know the song so well that we don't even need to look at the lyrics. We can just focus on the performance.

UNDERSTAND THAT THE HATERS GONNA HATE

As Taylor Swift reminds us, players gonna play, and haters gonna hate, but we need to learn to shake it off. To that point, let's unpack the three types of haters: so-called friends, critics, and direct opposition.

So-Called Friends

When we say "haters gonna hate," we are not just talking about sworn enemies. We are also talking about the people, sometimes even so-called friends, who respond to our success with jealousy and discouragement. These people aren't really our friends. Real friends want the best for us, and while they may challenge us, they will never discourage us from achieving the change we seek.

Jim recalls that a dear friend was one of the haters he encountered at the onset of his transformational change. It was someone close, who had no idea he was hating. The bomb he dropped came in one simple sentence: "Well, just make sure you don't dream too big." That may be the worst thing you can say to someone who is on his mark, ready to go. Yet this person had no idea what he was doing or saying.

Critics

If you're fortunate enough to reach or inspire the masses, there will be critics who, no matter how great your work is, will not like it and will cut you down. Expect it and be ready. When you have poured your heart and soul into something and are told that it's rubbish, it hurts. You can be hurt. That's normal. What you can't do is quit.

Whatever you are working on, it's not for everyone, and that's the plain and simple truth. When people don't like what you've created, your work, just remember it was not really for them. It was for the people with whom it resonated. As Jon Acuff says, we are all impacted by "critic math." Critic math, as Acuff explains, is a formula that goes like this: one thousand compliments plus one criticism equals one criticism. It is important to limit the number of opinions you embrace. Not everyone is going to connect to your version of Nickelback's "Arms Wide Open." (Yes, we know that was Creed, but now we know that *you* know that was Creed, and you will immediately be removed from our mailing list.) See? Even we can be haters.

Direct Opposition

Sometimes the hater will be someone who is radically opposed to the change you are called to and will actively try to stop it. Direct opposition comes in many shapes and sizes. It can be as obvious as a march in the streets or as elusive as a behind-the-scenes Washington lobbyist. As change-makers, we are passionate and convinced that the work we are engaged in is important. As a result, it can be hard to understand that some people don't see things the same way. It could be something as polarizing as gun owner rights and socialized medicine or simply a strong parental opposition to our career choice.

No matter what kind of hater we find ourselves up against, maintaining our commitments in the face of even the most difficult of circumstances is crucial. Also important is working to understand the critic's perspective and motivation. As Steven Covey famously stated, "We must seek first to understand and then to be understood." Identifying and understanding criticism allows us to move strategically and effectively forward, ever closer to the change we are attempting to create.

As a final word on haters and opposition, consider and find encouragement from this proverb: "A kite rises against the wind, not with it."

SHOWSTOPPERS

1. **Being underprepared:** Half-assed effort leads to half-assed results. Duane Cummings has lived a movie-worthy life. From playing professional soccer to owning a team franchise, from landing multi-million dollar deals to now becoming the CEO for Leadercast, facilitating the largest one-day convergence of leaders in the world by creating an epic leadership experience. From his days laced up in soccer togs to the boardroom, Cummings has learned that being prepared for what "could" happen gives him the competitive edge: "Filling the world with leaders who are worth following is amazing. I get to work around people that they walk through the door knowing that it's a blessing to go in there and serve. I can get compensated in a way that I feel valued. I'm serving people that want to be served. I'm not force-feeding somebody. I'm not giving somebody something they don't want. I probably spend, as a leader, 80 percent or 85 percent of my time preparing for things that will never happen. That's what we did as a coach. We used to practice man down, man up. We have a referee call all bad calls. We do all these things to prepare. No matter what change comes your way, it should actually feel natural. It should feel planned for. It should feel embraced."

2. **Motivation misaligned with your values:** If we don't connect to the "why," keeping our commitments becomes monumentally difficult.

3. **Comparing yourself to others' covers of the original:** Not everyone has performed a cover successfully. Some have crashed and burned. That doesn't mean you shouldn't perform the cover, nor does it mean you won't be successful. Your version is *your* version. Don't let the harrowing stories of others' attempts dissuade you from passionately performing your rendition.

ROCK STARS OF CHANGE: PAUL REDMOND

Few people in this world have negotiated conflict as well as Paul Redmond. We were thrilled and surprised when he agreed to an interview. Paul is no-nonsense kinda guy and doesn't suffer fools gladly. As head of counterintelligence for the CIA, he has literally seen it all during his storied thirty-three-year career.

Redmond was central to taking down CIA analyst turned KGB mole Aldrich Ames and was a recipient of the Distinguished Intelligence Medal, the Federal Order of Merit from the President of Germany, and the National Intelligence Distinguished Service Medal.

At Redmond's request, we meet mid afternoon in a townie bar, north of Boston, a bar hosting a handful of regulars drinking their late lunches and chatting the day away. Paul waits quietly at the far corner. His seat is the only one from which you can see the entire room. If this sounds like the start of a spy novel, that's because his life mirrors most fiction spy novels.

In person, Paul Redmond is affable and dressed as though he may have come from doing yard work. As we mic check for recording levels, he begins to chant in Latin and then chuckles. "Know what I just said?" he asks. "No, my Latin is pretty rusty," I reply. He then proceeds to tell me about how, when he was an altar boy in the Catholic Church, he and friends would chant inappropriate phrases during Mass to see if the priest would notice. His favorite was *May cacas in vestri caput super volucres quoque caeli latet*, or, "May the birds of the sky shit on your head." Both the priest and Redmond's father found it hysterical.

We first ask about how he found his Own Original Voice, and Redmond pipes in with, "I've always had it. For as long as I can remember, I've always had it." Paul's father, as noted in the altar boy story, encouraged Paul's humorous/rebellious side, instilling in him a confidence that enabled him to move forward when circumstances were challenging. Few know more about unintentional change than Paul Redmond, and yet, as we learn from his interview, in his world, effectiveness comes from expecting the unexpected.

"The problem with government work," Redmond shares, "is not so much about change but rather about getting things done. If there is a change, it's really going from not getting things done, to getting things done. You have to have a certain amount of arrogance when working with the government. I'd lecture new operatives and tell them, the only thing you're gonna get done in this place is in spite of it."

Part of Redmond's ability to get things done comes from zero tolerance for red tape. The core value that kept him in a job riddled with red tape might surprise you. When asked how he tolerated it, he indicated it was fun. He then quickly looks across the room as though transported to that time of his life and says, "I can't think of anything more fun than running espionage operations."

We mention to Paul that all the red tape, lives on the line, and the task of thwarting the KGB at the height of the Cold War seems more stressful than fun. He says, "It can be incredibly stressful. You worry about your spy getting caught or screwing things up." He makes the point that "stress needs to be compartmentalized." It's clear from Paul Redmond's recollection of his time with the agency that the fun outweighed the stress and that the little boy, brazen enough to try to make his parish priest laugh, was fueled, at least in part, by entertaining acts of rebellion. However, the rebellion contained both a child interested in mastering Latin and an adult who knew what it took to be an effective spy.

In his early days with the CIA, he had to do drops, jump from airplanes, and learn to use spy weapons. To understand the spy game, he needed to be able to do everything he would eventually have people under him do, but much better. In great detail, he breaks down the qualities you need to be an effective spy. The critical components, according to Redmond, include "training, experience, and intuition." The training, we learn, is extensive beyond imagination. Paul talks about how exhaustive intel and knowledge are essential. He says, "We knew so much about the KGB that we could predict with a certain amount of accuracy what they were up to. You can't get any of that from a book."

His segue way into intuition is fascinating: "Intuition is a function of knowledge, of knowing as much about the enemy/your subject as possible." He makes the point, "Sometimes you have to fly by the seat of your pants," and that's where a well-developed intuition is critical.

As we consider the theme of this book in light of our time with Paul Redmond, we see that training is all about the Cover Song Approach. New spies are taught tactics and skills and rehearse exacting details over and over again. They don't question; they just learn. When Redmond determined they were ready for the field, the Sample Song Approach was in full swing. At that point, it's a mix of who they are as individuals and the extensive training they have endured.

The Original Song approach is best illustrated in one of Redmond's own favorite spy stories: "We were running a technical operation against some really bad guys. We needed to be really close to their headquarters. We didn't even know where it was located when we got there, but we found it. Everyone else was in a big hurry. Behind their building was a jungle, and on one side, there was a house. But next to their building was a vacant lot. Without asking for permission or dealing with red tape, I had one of my operatives actually build a building. Right there, right next to it, I had my spies have a building built. My team came in from DC, did their thing, and it worked."

Without permission or engaging in red tape, Redmond has used his training, intel, and his intuition (OOV) to write an original song. In this case, the song was a building, and the Grammy Award was taking down a bunch of "really bad guys" without them ever seeing it coming.

Paul's work with the CIA required an extraordinary level of commitment. What if the building idea had turned out to be a catastrophe? What if it had cost lives? Redmond makes the point that "sometimes you have to be willing to put your ass on the line." What are you willing to risk in service of the change you desire?

THE BRIDGE

The Cover Song Approach is where we start the change process. It is the most natural way to create change and the easiest with which to connect. While it doesn't require any creativity, it is the perfect way to take the first step to the stage. It gets you on the right track and headed in the right direction. Instead of fretting over how we will approach the change we seek, finding the appropriate "cover song" allows us to begin by simply following pre-established instructions. Taking that first step is easier when we aren't responsible for coming up with "a plan." No matter what type of change you are facing, a "song" that you can perform has already been written.

However, there may well come a time when you grow tired of playing someone else's song. No matter how successful you have been in covering it, or even how many people loved your performance, once you have mastered a song, it is natural to dream about how you could make it better. This is the telltale sign that you are ready for our next approach to change: the Sampled Song Approach.

NEW AND IMPR"OOV"ED: THE SAMPLED SONG APPROACH

BUILDING A BETTER MOUSETRAP

"Sampling" is the process of taking a familiar piece of a cover song and using it to create another song. When a musician has mastered a cover, he can then choose to alter it in a way that makes it his own. What do Vanilla Ice and David Bowie have in common? Much to Bowie's chagrin, a bass line unites the two. "Ice Ice Baby" was a mega hit in 1989 for the infamous rap artist. Vanilla Ice created his hit by "sampling" the bass line from Queen and Bowie's 1981 song "Under Pressure," resulting in one of biggest hip-hop tracks in music history.

When we use the Sampled Song Strategy to approach change, we rely on the familiar part of an original piece of work to serve as a comfortable foundation on which to build. By adding our own contribution to the mix, we raise the risk and accountability slightly in exchange for a greater chance of personal accomplishment and meaningful impact.

The desire to build a better mousetrap has existed forever, or at least since the invention of mousetraps. In fact, we can see it in everything, from garden hoses to laundry detergent. It has even fueled the battle between fast food giants to serve the best burger.

Americans consume nearly fifty-billion burgers per year. Yes, billions. People pledge allegiance to Wendy's, Burger King, Five Guys, McDonalds, White Castle, Krystal, In-N-Out, or Hardee's—take your pick. Or your favorite burger may be your mom's or the Barefoot Contessa's, with a big knob of butter in the middle (it's a real thing.) No matter the version, did you know that each is merely a "sampled song" of a hit created by Louis' Lunch?

Louis' Lunch, in New Haven, Connecticut, is credited as the restaurant that invented the burger in 1895. Not only are they still in operation today, but they also continue to use the same antique, vertical cast iron gas stoves from 1898. You know about burgers, in part, because of

Louis' Lunch, but mostly because there was a person who ate one at some point in time and said, "I can do this better." And then another person said the same thing, and then, well, you get the point. Over one-hundred years later, the battle to make a better burger is still in full force.

LET'S GET GR"OOV"Y, BABY

The belief that we can offer something to improve an established song, process, or idea is born out of the discovery of our Own Original Voice (OOV). Artists spend a lifetime trying to find theirs. It's easier to emulate our favorite artists than to explore who we truly are. Being a "copycat" has far less risk, as we know people already love the artist we are mimicking. We then might want to tap into that love and claim it as our own.

This is exactly what record labels do when they are trying to bring a new artist to market. One of the first marketing campaigns is revealing who the new artist sounds like. "If you like Pearl Jam, you are going to love _____" is designed to pacify the threat of the uncertain and manage the far-too-common fear of the unknown. It identifies an act we know and love and then uses it to influence our decision to listen to the new artist.

Artist and Repertoire (A&R) reps for record labels will tell you that they are looking for "originality." But what they really are looking for is someone who pays homage to the successes of the past while adding a "new and improved" sticker to the box. This is what we, the audience, have been programmed to accept. How many times have we purchased something at the store solely because it had the "new and improved" label on it?

The Sampled Song Strategy to approaching change follows that same formula. We are taking something that has already been proven successful and adding our OOV while trying to improve on past results. For the corporate trainer, it's adding your OOV while teaching Covey's *7 Habits of Highly Effective People*. For the Jenny Craig follower, it's tweaking recipes and exercises so they better suit your lifestyle and goals. For the person starting a new job, it's bringing your own unique perspective to the role you now fill.

As a musician, the idea of sampling has always had a "cheaters" stigma to it. Someone is simply cashing in on the popularity of another's hit and then piggy-backing off the success, rather than creating something uniquely his own. This opinion is widespread and in fact is even held by the Grammy Award committee. If your song contains a sample in it, you are ineligible for the Song of the Year Grammy Award.

Generally speaking, we agreed with this policy. However, an incredible TED Talk from famed producer Mark Ronson ("Uptown Funk") changed our opinion. He explains it isn't about "hijacking nostalgia." Rather, it's about inserting yourself into the narrative of a song while also pushing that story forward. He uses the classic 80s hit from Doug E. Fresh and Slick Rick, "La Di Da Di," to provide an example of a song that has been sampled over five hundred times by everyone from Snoop Dog to Miley Cyrus. Each of these artists took the inspiration the song produced and added their OOV to bring something fresh and new, thus inspiring a younger generation to discover the legendary hip hop track.

🎸 ROCK STARS OF CHANGE: KEVIN LILLY, JR. 🎸

Which brings us to our interview with Kevin Lilly Jr., co-founder of Rock Brothers Brewing, who says, "I found my niche in the space between 'art and business.'"

That niche comes in the form of Rock Brothers Brewing. Rock Brothers unites craft beer and music in the type of experience that every fan longs for: the chance to authentically support and bond with their favorite bands. Rock Brothers partner artists are intimately involved in creating a craft brew their fans will embrace and enjoy. From recipe inception, brand creation, artwork design, and even the name of the product itself, the band is involved every step of the way. While the company is experiencing explosive growth with the success of partnerships, such as Hootie and the Blowfish's "Hootie's Home-grown Ale," it was a long and challenging road to get to their current "overnight success."

When Rock Brothers co-founder Kevin Lilly Jr. initially had an idea in 2006 to partner with some of his favorite bands to create craft beer, the path to making that happen was yet to be forged. Things needed to change before this type of partnership was possible.

We ask Kevin: "What was the most difficult change you went through?"

"The biggest challenge was taking knowledge of the music industry and converting that into a craft beer . . . The brand had to be received by both the fans of the artists and craft beer enthusiasts alike." According to Lilly, "If one side of the equation seemed disingenuous, then it wouldn't have worked. Craft beer folks won't drink a crap beer with a high-profile band's name on it, and if the bands were not authentically involved in the beer-making process, then the fans would see it as a gimmick."

Lilly continues to elaborate on the challenges: "Equally challenging was launching an unproven business model in the ever-changing, evolving, and shark-like craft-beer market we are seeing across the country . . . not only from more local competition but also from the giants in the industry attempting to stop the growth of craft beer. We are having to adapt rapidly and with precision almost on a monthly basis."

We then ask about adapting quickly in an environment where change can happen instantly and often: "How did you adapt to that change?"

"I think being a passion-driven entrepreneur and having that 'never quit, no matter the cost' mentality has been the driving force that is getting us through the tough terrain," says Lilly.

We ask about having to make decisions in the face of adversity: "Did the decisions you made have any unexpected consequences? If so, how did you address those?"

"Being in the brewing industry for the first time and having no experience has given us our lumps, no doubt. Early in our business, we would over-brew, over-estimate sales, and spend money needlessly, without knowing it until after the fact. All of these things result in a bottom line that, if it continued, would have crippled the company," Lilly vulnerably shares. "We addressed it by surrounding ourselves with people who were experts in that field. We didn't try to focus on the parts of the business we didn't excel at and stayed true to the things we were good at. It was hard to let pieces of the business go in the hands of others, but you certainly can't do it all yourself."

Coming up with such a unique idea and being able to distinguish yourself in a world currently obsessed with micro-brewing also proved challenging, so we ask Kevin, "How did you discover your Own Original Voice (OOV)?"

"I found my niche in the space between 'art and business.' As a musician and artist myself, I discovered that most musicians can't do the 'business side' of the band very well. Their artistic mind gets in the way of better business sense very often," Lilly says with a bit of laughter. "The reverse is also true. Straight-up business professionals usually don't understand anything about what makes an artist tick. I am able to speak both languages fluently enough to understand the artists' mentality and purpose while also realizing that we need to make a profit."

Kevin embraces the idea that Rock Stars of Change need to create something new. Working diligently on an idea for almost a decade has enabled him to finally see the fruit of his persistence. We wonder about the driving force that allows him to stay committed to being an original: "Was there a compelling event or reason why you decided to go do you own thing?"

"If I'm going to work this hard in my short life, it's going to be for me and my dream . . . not someone else's."

It is a powerful concept to write yourself into the narrative of something to which you emotionally connect, just like Kevin did. Adding our OOV to a proven hit allows us to efficiently overcome many common hurdles that prevent us from achieving change. So how do we find and engage our OOV? Exercising our OOV requires a few key elements. Let's look at those now.

EXERCISING YOUR OOV

Be A Subject Matter Expert

In order for us to have the swagger needed to share, we need to have a complete mastery of the subject. As indicated earlier, this takes time and commitment. True mastery can't be rushed or faked.

Jim remembers a recent situation where true mastery was essential: "My friends had lost their mother/grandmother. She was beloved by many, including me. Most of her family works in the music industry in one way or another. They're performers, producers, tour managers, and promoters. I mention that only to make the point that music means more to them than most. This family eats, sleeps, and breathes music. When they asked me to play at the memorial service, I was honored and, at the same time, a bit intimidated. The song they requested was written by a Canadian singer/songwriter named Bruce Cockburn. He is a guitar virtuoso, one of my musical heroes, and a friend of their family. The intimidation grew.

"'All the Diamonds' is a relatively simple song—except for the part that isn't. The 75 percent that's easy was no problem. I've been playing the guitar since seventh grade, so you'd think the tricky part wouldn't be that tricky. It was . . . It is . . . I was freaking out. I got the point where I'd play it perfectly three times in a row and then completely mess up on the fourth. It seemed like every time I felt comfortable, I'd make a mistake and my nerves would set back in. It had to be right. If you make a mistake during a concert, that's one thing. You can make a joke and shake it off. It happens. When it's your friend's mom's memorial service, there's no recovering.

"I had no room for rushing or faking and only one solid option: give it the time it required and commit to as much practice as it would take to master the song. I did exactly that. I must have played that run five hundred times. The goal was not just to play it correctly but to be so prepared that I would be able to feel it in the moment and translate that feeling meaningfully. She deserved that level of effort.

"The rehearsing was extensive and the practice tedious. I could have taken the easy way out and omitted the difficult portion. That idea was tempting, but I deemed it not an option. When I arrived at the church to bid farewell to a dear, sweet woman whose life had touched countless people, I was ready. The guitar felt good in my hands, and I was able to feel the words. In that moment, every bit of work I had put into that song was worth it."

Be Willing to Shift Perspective

As you master the cover, you no longer see the song through the eyes of a beginner. A beginner sees words and notes and battles discouragement and the pain of practicing. As Ralph Macchio learned in *The Karate Kid*, waxing cars and painting fences had a deeper meaning than simply performing chores around Mr. Miyagi's house. It wasn't until he had done those tasks ad nauseam and mastered the motions that Miyagi revealed their intended purpose. Ralph was suddenly able to block his teacher's punches and kicks without even thinking about it. Sometimes the work of a beginner seems pointless, but we are able to move to the next level only when the lessons behind the hard work become clear. A master has reached that point and sees what's beyond the surface; he is able to recognize and understand things like context and intention.

Be Clear in Your Intention

Allow your hard work to pay off in a way that has more impact than being the big shot at the karaoke bar. Use what you have learned to make a difference. A true Rock Star of Change knows where he's from and what he's learned, but then he uses his experience to define his intention. Understanding our intention allows us to effectively write ourselves into the narrative of any story (including our own) and fulfill the change we are compelled to create.

Be Passionate

While you may think it's your rock-solid understanding of the subject matter that people connect to, most connect more easily to passion. Passion compels others to pay attention, listen, and consider their own beliefs. Can you name one rock star who wasn't passionate? Exactly. Passion inspires. Whether you are thinking of Martin Luther King Jr. or Mark Cuban, it is undeniable that their OOV and passion created impactful change. From hundreds of thousands marching for equal rights to an average Joe watching *Shark Tank* and finding the courage to pursue an idea, passion motivates people to engage. This concept also applies to you. Tapping into your own passion will encourage you to share your OOV and keep your commitments toward the change you seek.

PERFECTING THE SAMPLED SONG APPROACH

Be Creative

Creativity is mysterious. It is born out of a mix of nothing and everything. The "everything" is made out of life experiences, memories, inspiration, and the things that move us. Sometimes the way in which those things come up is completely out of the blue. As writers, we have come to expect the unexpected. We know that when we are open to everything, we give everything the opportunity to show up. The "nothing" is simply the time and space we intentionally create for everything to come and make its grand entrance. The work of creativity is to shape without forcing.

When it comes to making impactful change, trusting our feelings and intuition is important. To brush off a deeply felt thought or idea is to miss the boat. Being creative allows for mistakes. This is why true creativity requires a level of vulnerability not present in the Cover Song Approach to change.

Be Vulnerable

Our additions to the song aren't always going to make it better, making the creative process both scary and counter intuitive. We are teetering on the brink of a profound cultural shift from generations where force and manipulation ruled to a new paradigm where the heart matters. When an artist is truly vulnerable, people are drawn into a place that inspires them to operate and communicate from a place that may have previously been off limits.

Maryann Williamson talks about this in her essay, "Our Greatest Fear": "Your playing small does not serve the world. There's nothing enlightened about shrinking so that other people won't feel insecure around you . . . As we let our own light shine, we unconsciously give other people permission to do the same."

When we give ourselves permission to operate from a place of vulnerability, we serve not only our own interests, but we also free and inspire others to do the same. As it relates to change, those who work from this place are unlikely to have to work alone.

Be Balanced

The first challenge in developing our OOV is learning how much of it to share with those around us. If we share too little, then our point of view and contribution can be overshadowed by the power of the material we are covering. If we share too much, then we risk losing what has made the cover a hit.

When Puff Daddy/Diddy wrote "I'll be Missing You," a tribute to the Notorious BIG, this balance was spot on. He took The Police hit "Every Breath You Take" and moved the story forward by paying honor to his fallen friend. This is exactly what Mark Ronson was referring to in his TED Talk. Diddy skillfully wrote himself into the narrative.

As we make room for our OOV in the Sampled Song Approach, we have to shift to an "indoor voice" as we search for balance. There will be plenty of room for getting loud in the next chapter (Original Song Approach).

SHOWSTOPPERS

> **Displaying over/under confidence:** Being overconfident is like wearing a giant shiny belt buckle that says "Douche." No one wants to see that. We also must warn you that being under confident is not a good approach either. You will present yourself as an amateur, making it difficult for anyone to take your OOV seriously.

> **Being a poser:** Posers have a skewed motive because they care so much about wanting to impress. They come off as fake, and their shallow obsession with popularity usually shows. Worse than misplaced confidence is questionable motivation.

Ignoring your instincts: True creativity, vulnerability, and balance require you to trust your gut. When you ignore your instincts, you ignore the things that make you an artist and agent of meaningful change.

⟞ ROCK STARS OF CHANGE: ROB BELL ⟝

As we work through each of these steps, we move closer to creating our OOV. Our interview with Pastor Rob Bell helps to demonstrate our point. In chapter 2, we introduced you to this game-changer, who sought to reclaim the sermon as an art form. We shared with Rob our plans to write a book, and he generously offered to answer questions and offer insight into his personal changes. We were particularly interested in finding out how and when he became aware of his desired change. He describes this moment: "[It happened in] June 1992. First sermon. In the woods at a religious service for people who worked at a camp. It was a dodgy one, for sure. Me spouting off on something I found in the Bible. I laugh now at the audacity."

As admittedly dodgy as his first sermon was, he goes on to say, "It grabbed me. Interestingly enough, what struck me most was (A) This is what I'm here to do. And (B) I might really be terrible at this, but it would get me out of the bed in the morning, and I'd enjoy it. Fascinating, isn't it?"

We did indeed find Rob's answer fascinating. As musicians, we both started out with stars in our eyes. But we also know the realization that you're unlikely to become a superstar is what causes most people to quit. For us, we fell in love with music as we simultaneously realized we were never going to become Bono. For Rob, he started out pretty sure he wouldn't become a rock star, and then he did, though it seems like he may not realize it even now. Keep in mind that Rob Bell has been considered by *Time* to be among the one hundred most influential people in the world; he is also a *New York Times* bestselling author several times over. But as it relates to "making it," he says, "Success wasn't even on the radar. It still isn't, really."

Bell has a unique approach to speaking and writing. We assumed, at least in the early days, that there must have been a preacher who inspired him stylistically. We were hoping for a funny, nostalgically embarrassing memory about how he practiced being Billy Graham in his bedroom mirror, preaching into a hairbrush microphone. That apparently never happened. As it relates to the preachers he wanted to copy or be like, he says, "I didn't have any. There was one preacher I greatly admired who I went to work for because I knew I had a ton to learn from him, but I didn't see myself copying anyone. That's why I got into it. I didn't see anyone doing it how I thought it should be done. Which, of course, [now] sounds incredibly arrogant."

It's not that others didn't inspire Bell. Rather, he comments that he admires a "long list of people who had found their voice"—a list made up of "musicians, comedians, philosophers, and designers who were using what they had in compelling ways." He cites people like comedian Eddie Izzard, Pete Garrett from Midnight Oil, writer Ken Wilbur, and producer/musician Les Claypool as some of the people who shaped him. This is where the line between the Cover Song and Sampled Song Approach blurs. The inspiration, application, and manifestation of what Bell was trying to accomplish seems to exist in a simultaneous mix of all three approaches.

In light of this mix, we asked Rob about the process of finding his OOV. His answer is candid: "Lots of bombing. Seriously, trying something and it not working, not clicking, not connecting. And then driving home humbled and curious, wondering why some things had fire and some went down in flames." According to Bell, the key is "always, always, always trying the next thing." Bell continues by saying, "That's the only way it works. You just keep going, keep getting back up, keep giving it another shot." Bell beautifully proves that change, as we have shared, is not an all or nothing proposition. The road to change is sometimes littered with shrapnel.

On the origin of his commitment level, Rob says, "I had no other option, no other plan, no other ideas of what to give myself to. It was the sermon. Reclaiming this ancient art form for whoever wanted to listen." He describes his process as "creating space where people could wake up. It's still what I do. And I'm more compelled than ever by the work."

It is clear that the same things that compelled him over twenty-five years ago still drive Rob. He concludes by saying, "It's about following the curiosity wherever it leads—a deeply personal quest, hunt, like pursuing a line of inquiry. You go where the questions take you. And you get some answers which, of course, lead you to new questions."

It is in Bell's compulsive curiosity that his body of work has resulted in an ever-unfolding original "song." His openness, courage, and resourcefulness, combined with an unwavering commitment to his mission, give him true rock star status.

THE BRIDGE

When we use the Sampled Song Approach for change, we add in our OOV to the song to keep us engaged and provide new opportunities for creativity. With creative contribution comes an increased level of ownership and, ultimately, more accountability. This approach is perfect for the game-changers who realize they have something important to say but still need a little support. It provides us with a greater chance to achieve the change we seek.

Finding the confidence to add our OOV to the mix and being willing to face the potential failure it could bring are steps toward becoming the elusive "original" artist that all true rock stars are. This is a passionate pursuit and one where our passion grows as we experience the power of our OOV made manifest. The Sampled Song Approach is the middle ground between where we started and where we are ultimately headed, which brings us to our final approach to change.

Contributing creatively is addictive. It's like getting your first tattoo or eating a breadstick at the Olive Garden. Before you know it, you're already dreaming about the next one. When the creative addiction takes over, we cross the bridge to becoming a true original artist and develop an increased level of potential influence. Grab your leather pants. It's time to rock.

THE ORIGINAL SONG APPROACH

UNSATISFIED AND INSPIRED

To this point, we have used cover songs and sampling as metaphors for approaching change. But the Original Song Approach is a bit different. This approach not only takes into consideration the obvious stepping stones needed to learn the basic steps and discover our OOV, but it also invites anyone serious about powerful change to gather all she has learned, engage her own, fresh voice, and step onto the stage to bare her soul for the audience.

NEED, INSPIRATION, ACTION, COMMITMENT

Your original song begins with an unsatisfied need or longing. The old adage "necessity is the mother of invention" fuels the Original Song Approach, causing us to look for solutions in unexpected, unconventional places. Because your approach may seem crazy to the rest of the world, original game-changers have always had to ignore or silence the naysayers. Be prepared and allow your inner burn to ignite an unstoppable pursuit and pave the way for inspiration.

Everyone understands that necessity gives birth to invention, but no one talks about what happens between getting pregnant and actually having the baby. Necessity impregnates inspiration, but the baby might not be born if inspiration's job ended right then and there. Inspiration must lead to action for it to be of value.

In the 1890s, a massive flood hit a small village near Saigon. While the damage that surging water can cause is enough to decimate a small village, that was the least of their problems. The rising water brought with it monocled cobras. *Frickin cobras!* The venomous snakes bit over forty people, eventually killing four of them.

French physician, Albert Calmette, living at the time in what is now Vietnam, saw people dying and was inspired to lend a helping hand. He caught several of the snakes, extracted their venom, and injected it into horses to create antibodies. He then drew the horses' blood to use as a serum and created an antivenom that saved many human lives. It doesn't get more rock 'n' roll than cobras, and Dr. Calmette was a total badass rock star. There was a need, and that need inspired Calmette to take action. This story is just one example of what an original approach looks like.

Inspiration is born out of a desire for change. Think of how we listen to music. As we write in 2017, the idea of putting a compact disc into a machine seems almost antiquated. Someone wanted to carry his entire music library in his pocket and figured out how to send music into space and then shoot it back into a tiny device that allows musicians and listeners alike to offer and receive music anywhere in the world, instantly. The goal was about making music easy to share and obtain. Forget about the impact on the music industry or how righteous vinyl sounds for a moment. For now, simply focus on the seeming impossibility of making this happen and the fact that you now see this technological change as common.

AS WE WERE WRITING THIS CHAPTER, THE NEWS BROKE THAT THE MP3 FORMAT OF CODING SONGS IS GOING AWAY. TECHNOLOGY HAS ONCE AGAIN MADE A CUTTING-EDGE PROCESS ANTIQUATED. THE RISE OF STREAMING SERVICES LIKE SPOTIFY AND PANDORA HAS LED TO THE CREATION OF NEW FORMATS LIKE AAC THAT PROVIDE BETTER AUDIO QUALITY. RIP, MP3. YOU HAD A GOOD RUN. WE EXPECT THAT SOMEONE READING ROCK 'N' ROLL WITH IT TWENTY YEARS FROM NOW WILL GET A CHUCKLE OUT OF THIS SECTION. BY THEN, THE CHIPS WILL HAVE ALREADY BEEN IMPLANTED IN EVERYONE'S BRAIN, AND WE WILL SIMPLY THINK, "I WANT TO HEAR BARRY MANILOW RIGHT NOW," AND "COPACABANA" WILL PLAY. SOME GUY LIVING IN HIS PARENTS' GARAGE WILL BE LISTENING TO ARCADE FIRE ON A CD PLAYER, TALKING ABOUT HOW HE LIKES TO KICK IT OLD SCHOOL. HIPSTERS OF THE FUTURE, UNITE.

Sometimes an experience motivates our Original Song Approach. You've tried the cover song and sampling approaches, but nothing made a difference. To find the solution you desire, you may need to look deep inside yourself for information that Google or Jenny Craig might not offer.

It can be incredibly discouraging when a cover song that has worked for millions doesn't work for you. This is where most people give up and, ultimately, give in to what they perceive are insurmountable circumstances. Giving up is a choice, but not if you want to achieve great things. Consider Nelson Mandela and the odds he faced in South Africa. Change seemed impossible, yet he refused to let circumstance overwhelm him. On release from his twenty-seven-year prison sentence, he said, "As I walked out the door toward the gate that would lead to my freedom, I knew if I didn't leave my bitterness and hatred behind, I'd still be in prison."

No Cover or Sample Song Approach can overcome twenty-seven years of imprisonment for political or philosophical ideologies. There was no support group, book, or program for Nelson Mandela to reference. However, he had a choice as to how he would respond. No matter what, he was not going to carry his bitterness and hatred with him. In order for him to stay committed to his life's mission, he chose to let this go. Often, simply realizing that we have a choice is the most powerful fuel for truly original personal change. Just because we don't see a solution, it doesn't mean there isn't one.

Speaking of choices, we have another choice to make if we are going to use the Original Song Strategy. We have to choose to let go of "perfection." The alarming latest studies on perfectionism reveal the potentially devastating, destructive consequences of chasing utopia. Psychologist Thomas Greenspon recently published a paper in *Psychology in the Schools* in which he claims, "Research confirms that the most successful people in any given field are less likely to be perfectionistic, because the anxiety about making mistakes gets in your way."[4] We need the freedom to pursue creativity without the chains of unattainable, ideological intentions.

[4] http://onlinelibrary.wiley.com/doi/10.1002/pits.21797/epdf?referrer_access_token=t5JiXZ8OrspLD2pmyLb-FE4keas67K9QMdWULTWMo8OSGFL qu3VMh9l9Pn1yUqDVE06H-s90Co8JEvsaJy9lpAS30yv0Iidc3PXlQKHrZ-uEBmtN1f7KjZsGVMnX9l_S8uJE2vd5FqSBMLMp7unrdqQLvmSltOY-Xb4hian15PSs7eGhF-ylYjoMKSxUVfdLvRP08U92USxC5YgEIJeL5-HfMtVsP4ciiNJdClU_gLu8GMlXNusjvJ0rnHD7s--M

BEAUTIFUL IMPERFECTION

Jackson Pollock was once asked how long it took him to paint a particular painting. He looked at the person asking and said, "My whole life." For us, we have started this chapter over and over again. We have written, deleted, re-written, and deleted. It is impossible for us to write about originality and creativity without acknowledging the allure of striving for perfection.

In 2003, Brant had the opportunity to play the Greenbelt Arts and Music Festival in Cheltenham, England. Greenbelt is a legendary event where art, faith, music, and justice collide in the most incredible of ways. Since its inception in 1974, the festival has had artists like U2, Moby, Midnight Oil, Michael Franti, Bruce Cockburn, Martyn Joseph, Randy Stonehill, The Polyphonic Spree, Aqualung, and others grace its eclectic stages. It has grown from its humble beginnings of a few hundred people to over twenty thousand over the bank holiday weekend each year.

The "godfather" of this festival is a man named Pip Wilson. Pip is a legendary character who is the heart and soul of Greenbelt. He worked with the YMCA for over four decades helping to transform impressionable young people into "beautiful human people," as he likes to call them. While at the festival, a small group of incredible humans would gather each year to refuel their empty spiritual tanks with hope and wonder and search for the possibility of experiencing the type of transformation that leaves an impact on the world around them.

As Brant recalls, "We sat around the fireplace in the hotel lobby to the wee hours of the morning after each day at the festival and got lost in majestic conversation, like we were kids hiding in a blanket fort, discussing how we were going to take over the world. It was on one of these whiskey-fueled nights that Pip talked about the world's obsession with perfection. It is an epidemic. He used this great metaphor of standing in a hallway gazing upon a beautiful painting hanging slightly askew. Most of the world only sees the imperfection of the crooked frame and never actually recognizes the beautiful painting it contains. Wow! Not only did this conversation open my eyes to this obsession, but it also made me realize that I was one of the people compulsively trying to correct the view. It inspired me to write the title track, "Beautiful Imperfection," to my band Fort Pastor's major label debut:

An old oil canvas it hangs crooked on the wall
Blindingly obvious from where I stand
Temptation to straighten the view from the hall
Missing the beauty of the artist's hand
You can pick it apart and look for correction
Try to find a better reflection
Maybe you should question your obsession
What you missed it was beautiful imperfection
Two lovers walking, playing tag with I love yous
It shouldn't be so hard to understand
Instead we judge them for the partners that they choose
Missing the beauty of the artist's hand
You can pick it apart and look for correction
Try to find a better reflection
Maybe you should question your obsession
What you missed it was beautiful imperfection
What they say is that beauty's in the eye of the . . .
What they say is that beauty's in the eye of the . . .
What they say is that beauty's in the eye of the . . .
You can pick it apart and look for correction
Try to find a better reflection
Maybe you should question your obsession
What you missed it was beautiful

Perfection looks down on originality because originality, in all its glory, is flawed. Flaws are the sworn enemy of perfection. Learning to see and accept the fact that we are imperfect *and* beautiful is a life-changing thought. It is incredibly freeing to let go of perfection, but even reading those words makes perfectionists twinge. Perfectionists shy away from doing things they think they won't be good at. They want to stay within the safety of the world they have crafted for themselves, yet this limits our chances of achieving impactful change.

We proudly refer to ourselves as "imperfectionists." The difference between perfection and imperfection is that imperfection actually exists. Rarely does a perfectionist tell you she did something amazing. More often than not, she uses the perfectionism as an excuse for not getting something done. Or, in many cases, she uses perfectionism as an excuse not to even try at all. As it relates to change, if you are waiting for something to be perfect, it will never see the light of day.

If we are going to be an original, we have to find the courage to try new things, stick with them long enough to become proficient, and then accept a certain amount of imperfection. Yet this type of wholehearted acceptance is not natural for most of us. It will stretch us as men, women, spouses, mothers, fathers, children, and humans. For some, it is monumentally difficult to resist the need to be perfect. These perfectionists may need to take the gloves off and bare-knuckle brawl with it until they are a bloody mess. Deeply satisfying change sometimes leaves us with broken bones and bruises. But if we stick it out and learn to see the beauty in imperfection, our cuts and bruises will heal, and the scars left behind will become signs of the "original" path we have traveled.

The Original Song Approach uses the Cover Song and Sampled Song as inspiration to craft a completely new song. It takes the collective strengths of what you have learned up to this point and then tips the scale toward originality by making unique choices. Thus, it can allow you to express yourself in a way only you can. This approach works best in two different scenarios.

The first scenario is that you have mastered the cover song, crushed the sample song, and have a head full of ideas as to how to improve your results beyond what you have already accomplished. It becomes a near obsession to get these ideas out of your head and into action.

The second scenario uses your struggles to motivate you toward originality. If you have tried the previous approaches with little to no

success, you might find the inspiration to carve a new path. Originality requires a whole new level of vulnerability. You must hold yourself
accountable to doing things differently than you have up to this point
to see a different result.

You have heard countless people say, "We are all our own worst
critic." The fact is, it's easy to point out flaws. Something inside many
of us would secretly love to be Simon Cowell on *American Idol*, hand-
ing down the truth from the judges' table. We all long for honesty and
truth at our core, but the notion that it has to take the shape of uncon-
structive, crippling criticism has become an unsettling cultural norm.
You certainly can be your own worst critic, if that's what you choose,
but we have a better option to offer you.

What if becoming an original was fueled by the notion that you are
in fact your greatest cheerleader, encourager, and even friend? Dare we
suggest you become your own biggest fan? A fan is a person enthusiastically devoted to something or somebody, such as a band, a sports
team, a book, or an entertainer. A true and devoted fan will go to great
lengths to show her loyalty. She will pay exorbitant amounts of money
for tickets, wear her team colors, and rearrange her schedule to make
sure she doesn't miss the game or concert, all to show support to those
she loves. When is the last time you treated yourself this way? When
was the last time you carved out time to work on fulfilling your mission? What if you spent the same amount of time and money on your
own personal development as you did on those playoff tickets?

Rock stars are often, for good reason, seen as egomaniacs. While
too much ego certainly has the potential to turn anyone into a grade-
A douchebag, maintaining a balanced, healthy ego enables us to
achieve what we desire. Rock stars encourage, believe in, and invest
in themselves.

While balance is, indeed, important, many of us have tipped the
scale in the direction of self-discouragement. Consider for a moment
the thing you long to change. Now imagine you are sitting with a
seven-year-old with the same big dreams. What might you say to him?
A single encouraging voice can be as powerful as a stadium filled with

people chanting your name, particularly if that single voice is your own. But back to the seven-year-old for just a minute. What would you actually say? What questions would emerge, born out of the sincere curiosity that arises from hearing about the goal, dream, or desire he's shared?

The Original Song Approach is really about tipping the scale from inner critic to inner fan. This requires a kind of reprogramming that, at first, might seem foreign or even uncomfortable. Two simple questions have the power to invite your inner fan to the show:

1. What kind of feedback/encouragement is helpful to you when you get it from outside sources?

2. What kind of feedback/encouragement do you offer others when they are looking for support?

Applying those words, phrases, and feelings to ourselves is a game changer.

THREE STEPS TO PERFECTING THE ORIGINAL SONG APPROACH

Be Open

True creativity and inspiration are mysterious and often don't make sense at first. The spark may come as a fleeting idea or a sense you can't explain. It could be as simple as how the intermittent wiper idea hit Robert Kearns or as revolutionary as listening to music that has been shot at you from outer space. Learning not to dismiss ideas, urges, or feelings allows you to create room to make the seemingly impossible, possible.

Be Resourceful

True game-changers are not deterred by a lack of resources. Rather, they make full use of what *is* available. Often, would-be change agents are waiting for someone to step up and meet a need, inspiring them to get started as well. The truth is that others are most likely to get involved when they see what you've accomplished with what you had to work with at the beginning. The biggest record deals ever signed were from bands that didn't need them. They figured out how to be successful on their own.

Be Committed/Courageous

Courage is a word we usually reserve for military, first responders, law enforcement, or firefighters—those who put themselves at risk for the sake of others. We need to view originality with that same reverence and admiration, striving to find the courage to say what needs to be said. We need the courage to swim upstream and wear our hearts on our sleeves for all to see, like full-arm tattoos. Thus, we will save ourselves from living a life of "less than" or "average."

The world is filled with things we have "settled for." How many people do you know who are stuck in a dead-end job because they think that's all they are qualified for? How many marriages do you see where someone has "settled" for a spouse who isn't her soul mate because she thinks she can't do any better? Rock stars don't settle for anything.

Taking risks and stepping out is no easy task. There will, no doubt, be a whole host of obstacles, unforeseen circumstances, and outside opinions to deal with. We must stay committed to achieving the change we seek. Courage and commitment, when manifested, enable us to believe in our vision and calling. Courage and commitment are what keep us from giving up.

SHOWSTOPPERS

Quitting: Without hitting you with a lame inspirational quote like, "Quitters never win," we will tell you that a true rock star has the swagger to carry on, no matter how bad the show was. Embrace the lessons that come from struggle. Use them as motivation to improve. Quitting because we can't hack it is different than thoughtfully choosing to pursue another approach. Rather than take our ball and go home, let's take the ball and try another way to score.

Negativity: Having a negative attitude is like wearing blinders that only allow us to see the problem but not a meaningful solution. Great ideas are crushed under the weight of pessimism, so we are prescribing a "power of positive thinking" ideology. To solve a problem, the problem needs to be acknowledged and understood, but the true Rock Star of Change doesn't stop there; he optimistically searches for the solution.

Stubbornness: This is a tricky one. The line between committed and foolish is thin. While we need a certain amount of dedication, flexibility and adaptability are also essential when using an original approach. We are often more concerned with being right than being effective. If being effective in service of your desired change is really important, you will at least acknowledge reason as reasonable and include cold, hard facts in your pursuit.

While the desire to be original is noble, pursuing originality for the sake of novelty is not. As C. S. Lewis once said, "No man who bothers about originality will ever be original: whereas if you simply try to tell the truth you will, nine times out of ten, become original without ever having noticed it." Being original is about fully embracing and applying our OOV through a palpable vulnerability. It's being comfortable with ourselves as we are and not trying be someone we are not. Authenticity is the key.

Now that we have learned the three approaches to change and how to use them, we need to sit in the green room, warm up our voices, tune our instruments, and get ready to take the stage.

THE GREEN ROOM

For a diehard fan, it is a dream come true to score a backstage pass to see his favorite musician. He's finally gonna get to chill with his favorite band, throw back a couple of cold ones, and ask every question he's ever thought of. In his mind, once the band finally meets him, they are going to be friends forever. But little does he know, the mysterious back stage realm is in reality pretty boring. No one is hanging out and just kicking it. If you are back there, it's because you're working. If you're a fan with a backstage pass, you are probably part of a "meet and greet," where you'll get forty-five seconds for a picture, an autograph, and a very quick hello. Beyond that, a fan could spend hours backstage and not even catch a glimpse of a rock star.

The promised land you actually seek is called the "green room." Sadly, you can't go in there. But, wait, my pass says "All Access," you might scream to oversized security guards. Yup, it sure does. But it should say everywhere *but* the green room. The green room, like the holy of holies in King Solomon's temple, is sacred territory. It also brings up the following question: What does a rock star do for the few hours before the show? Meditate? Stretch? Enjoy a few lustful moments in groupie heaven?

True rock stars are spending that time alone, coming up with the most effective way to provide their audiences with a transformational experience. They are writing out the set list to determine the order of songs they are going to play and looking for places in the show where they can create memorable moments. Ultimately, they are mapping out the emotional musical journey on which they plan to take their audience. Every artist has her own unique way of preparing for the show. But, in the end, the goal is the same: to enthusiastically create engaged and impacted super fans.

One of the biggest challenges of successfully navigating change is that, for all intents and purposes, the performer and the audience are one and the same. While we are responsible for executing the change that we seek, we also have to keep ourselves engaged in the process. This requires that we know when we are "losing the audience" and when to shift gears to keep ourselves completely and utterly engaged. How do we do that?

The short answer is that it is in this preparation that we realize the rock star is also a member of the audience. The musician has to offer something he would personally appreciate as a listener. If musicians only think about themselves as performers, they might have a self-indulgent good time, but not get much of a response. So the key here is embracing both perspectives. That is what a true rock star is capable of accomplishing.

Now, think of change like a concert. If we played the same song over and over again, it would make for a pretty frustrating evening. The same is true with change. If we approach change with only one strategy, our chances of truly engaging in change are limited. It becomes the classic "been there, done that" situation.

If we don't succeed, we accept our failure as absolute and forget there may be other strategies to accomplish our goal. Like a great concert, the process of change is dynamic, and the tactics must be diverse. Thus, to arrive at our desired outcome, we are going to need to combine and organize every one of the strategies we have learned to this point. This needs to be done in a way that is both exciting for the performer and compelling for the audience.

To remain engaged in the change we seek, we have to get in the "green room" and thoughtfully consider how to approach putting together our set list. When a musician accomplishes this, she is thinking of a few specific things, which we will now discuss.

THE AUDIENCE

A true rock star understands that different audiences require different songs. Playing your high-energy rock show at the public library for its patrons may not connect like you want it to. We need to consider for whom we are playing *before* we add songs to the set. When the audience is "us," we need to find the courage to be brutally honest with ourselves. Our level of self-awareness will directly affect our chances of success. To be honest, we need to ask ourselves:

1. What level of commitment is realistic in my current state of mind?
2. What are my current circumstances, and what do I seek to change?

If we can be honest about our mindset and appetite for change, it will help us tailor a set list that will resonate within. Remember, we have more than one song or approach to use in accomplishing our goal. It is okay if, at the moment, we can't give the level of commitment we want. We simply recognize that and adjust our set list accordingly. What does that mean?

Let's say we are not in a position to fully engage our OOV and dive into the Original Song Approach. So, we take a step back, recognize this truth, and then, perhaps, go with the tried and true Cover Song Approach until circumstances change. Remember that successfully accomplishing the change we seek requires us to weather the wait until change takes root. This is why we have more than one approach. If we need to sit back and follow pre-determined instructions for a while, that is totally okay. Intently watching "the audience" helps us know when to change approaches to keep them from disengaging.

TRANSITIONS

When attending and watching a concert, the difference between a pro and an amateur is most visible in between songs. An amateur will fumble through transitions, awkwardly trying to find something to say. A rock star will have thought through all of the transitions and use that time to engage the audience in a personal and authentic way. When we are attempting to bring forth change, we need to think through the transitions between the three approaches.

If we lived in a perfect world and could take a linear approach to change, then we would simply start with the Cover Song Approach, recognize when we have some thoughts of our own to incorporate, shift to the Sampled Song Approach, and continue to develop our

OOV until we build up the courage to fully embrace the Original Song Approach. Sounds easy, right? As we well know, our world is anything but perfect or easy.

In reality, life happens at such a frantic pace that switching back and forth between approaches is not only probable, it's necessary. Our focus is often torn in many directions with the start of each new day. If we simply try to follow the linear approach in the midst of life's storms, we will inevitably find ourselves disengaging from the process for a myriad of reasons—all of which are valid feelings in the moment. This is where we fall into the trap of allowing our feelings to drive our decisions. How do we avoid this and keep our values in the forefront while also recognizing how we feel in the moment?

As any real rock star will tell you, being fully prepared to perform allows you to "roll with it" when things don't go as planned. Unintentional change has a way of showing up at the worst possible moment. However, if we plan on it and have options to pivot toward another approach, then we can successfully navigate away from rushed, emotionally charged decisions and guide ourselves toward real solutions instead.

As Brant tells it, "Jim and I were facilitating a session for a client with Banding People Together. We had reached the end of the day and had just performed the songs we had written with our teams. The energy was high, and people were in a collaborative euphoria. We didn't have access to a full band with the ability to turn up the volume and take the energy to an even higher level with a closing song. If we tried to simply use the two microphones and couple of acoustic guitars we had, the moment would have fallen completely flat. But the crowd was hooting and hollering and clearly wanted more.

"Jim looked at me, walked out into the crowd, and stood on a chair. He strummed his guitar, unplugged, and looked out over the crowd. They slowly stopped clapping, and Jim invited them to come close as he played 'All You Need Is Love' by the Beatles. As he sang, the crowd swayed and sang along. Jim was able to transition them away from raucous excitement toward a truly powerful, memorable moment, with nearly a hundred voices coming together in a show of unity. That is what they will remember."

Someone unprepared for a moment like that would have tried to use the two available microphones and would have strummed his guitars as hard as he could. It would have been a lackluster way to end the day and, ultimately, a forgetful last performance. Jim took a completely different approach and kept the crowd engaged. He pivoted perfectly at a crucial moment, and the audience followed him like he was the Pied Piper. He was able to close the day with a powerful moment of vulnerability and the impact of True Collaboration™.

Understanding the tools you have been given thus far in this book is crucial to creating your own set list, which we will help you accomplish in the final chapter of this book.

THE WORKBOOK

Change, as we have we have indicated, is universal and constant. The process of "overcoming the challenge of change," however, is personal. Our goal in writing this book was not only to change the way we think about change but also to provide useful tools for both creating and responding to it.

For this section, think of the hits as the easy, quick answers that pop into your head. They may be the stories you've been telling yourself for years about why you can't move forward. But, here we invite you to listen to the whole album of your heart and mind, with the hope that you will discover what lies beneath the surface—the deep cuts, if you will.

The following questions and exercises are intended to serve as a framework into which you can insert your OOV. Take your time and be intentional about the time you take. Some of our favorite songs never became hits. Consider the words of Rumi: "Let yourself be silently drawn by the strange pull of what you really love. It will not lead you astray."

We encourage you to do this work in a quiet place where you feel grounded and undistracted. We also recommend having your calendar handy. We have defined success as making and keeping commitments, so along the way, we will be asking you to schedule commitments. Please, resist any temptation to skip questions. When you don't know, allow yourself to sit in that space and see what comes up. Write down whatever comes to mind, even if it doesn't make sense in the moment.

Listen, we know what you are doing right now. You are flipping through the next several pages, rolling your eyes, and saying something along the lines of, "Like I have time for this?!" You wouldn't have the potential to be a true rock star if you weren't feeling that way. But, here's the thing: to achieve lasting change, you can't take the shortcut. Not even once. We have tried. We have failed. We have written this frickin' book, for crying out loud! You don't have to do this in one pass. In fact, you shouldn't. So, take these questions in bite-sized pieces. It will be worth it. We promise.

For those about to rock (change), we salute you.

FACING CHANGE: DISCOVERING YOUR VISION

1. Change and hope are intertwined. What change do you hope to make or respond to? (Keep in mind that the response to unintentional change requires intention.)

2. Is the change intentional or unintentional?

3. Why is this particular change important to you?

4. If the change you are facing is unintentional:
   i.   What is the immediate threat level?
   ii. What is the situation surrounding the change?
   iii. What are your options for responding?

5. At this point, you need to convert the unintentional change to an intentional response. If the change you are facing is intentional:
   i.   What is the vision you have for this change?
   ii. What are the incremental goals you have established?
   iii. How are you going to measure your progress?

Remember, we define success as making and keeping commitments. This allows us to repeatedly celebrate successes while also quickly accepting accountability when commitments are broken.

BUILDING A STRONG "ROCK" STANCE: DEFINING YOUR VALUES

1. Who are your real-life heroes, with qualities you would want to model in your own life? What do you admire about them? List three adjectives to describe the heroes who come to mind.

    i. _____

    ii. _____

    iii. _____

2. What is your favorite film? Is there a particular character you relate to? Why? List three adjectives to describe the characters that come to mind.

    i. _____

    ii. _____

    iii. _____

3. Choose two or three moments in your life that you hold as a true "peak experiences." What were they? What made them so special? List three adjectives to describe who you were in those moments.

    i. _____

    ii. _____

    iii. _____

4. From the following list of values on the next page, choose three currently embody and three you are deficient in.

    i. _____

    ii. _____

    iii. _____

VALUES

AUTHENTICITY	ACHIEVEMENT	ADVENTURE	AUTHORITY
AUTONOMY	BALANCE	BOLDNESS	COMPASSION
CHALLENGE	CITIZENSHIP	COMMUNITY	COMPETENCY
COLLABORATION	CREATIVITY	CURIOSITY	DETERMINATION
FAIRNESS	FAITH	FAME	FRIENDSHIPS
FUN	GROWTH	HAPPINESS	HARMONY
HONESTY	HUMOR	INFLUENCE	INTEGRITY
JUSTICE	KINDNESS	KNOWLEDGE	LEADERSHIP
LEARNING	LOVE	LOYALTY	OPTIMISM
PEACE	PLEASURE	RECOGNITION	RESPECT
RESPONSIBILITY	SECURITY	SELF-RESPECT	SERVICE
SPIRITUALITY	STABILITY	SUCCESS	TRUST

OTHER: _____

5. From the first four questions in this section, make a list of the adjectives/values that came up. (There should be about a dozen.) Rank them in order of importance and then explain how you are currently honoring them and/or how you are not currently honoring them. By "currently" we are talking about the last four to six weeks.

6. Without judgment, use the list below to determine your primary and secondary motivations behind your intended change. Remember, our **PERCEPTION** of possible consequences influences our actions as much as the consequences we experience:

   i. **REMOVAL:** Are you doing this to avoid an aversive experience? What is that experience?

   ii. **INTERPERSONAL:** Are you doing this for someone other than yourself? Do I want them to influence my actions? In what ways?

   iii. **SENSATIONAL:** Are you doing this because it feels good to you? Are you depriving yourself from a positive personal sensory experience? How?

   iv. **MATERIAL:** Are you doing this to achieve a physical/material objective? If yes, what?

7. If you choose to ignore or abandon the area of change you are currently working toward, what impact will that decision have on you, your family, your community, and the world?

APPROACHING CHANGE: DECIDING WHAT SONG TO PLAY

Now that we have some answers, let's look at the different approaches we can use to accomplish the change we seek.

The Cover Song Approach

Answer the following questions as you think about developing your Cover Song Approach:

1. What are some of the "cover songs" that already exist that you could use to approach the change you are facing? (Preconceived programs, approaches, and processes that, if adhered to, are thought to yield results.)

2. What are some of the things you can do to ensure you perform these songs with passion and intention?

3. Who are the potential "haters" who will try to derail you? What are several ways you can respond to those people?

The Sampled Song Approach:

Answer the following questions as you think about developing your OOV:

1. How will you become a subject matter expert on the approach you are using?

2. How will you shift your perspective beyond that of a beginner?

3. What would you add or alter to the Cover Song Approach that would result in creating a Sample Song Approach?

4. What is the intention behind adding your voice?

5. Why are you passionate about it?

6. How will you be creative in your approach?

7. What is the worst thing that could happen by adding your OOV to the mix?

8. How will you know how much of your voice to add to the mix?

The Original Song Approach

Answer the following questions as you think about developing your Original Song Approach:

1. What about the previous approaches (Cover/Sample Song) leaves an unsatisfied longing and why?

2. For each of those items, list what you would add in its place.

3. For each addition, list one or two values you are honoring.

4. Who will you run your ideas past for critique and when?

5. How will you test each idea and when? (This is where you pull out your calendar and commit to trying your idea on for size.)

6. How are you preparing to let go of perfection as you pursue solutions?

7. In the spirit of being your own greatest fan, what kind of feedback and encouragement is helpful when you get it from outside sources?

8. What kind of feedback and encouragement do you offer others when they are looking for support?

9. List five things you love most about how you are dealing with the change you seek.

10. How are you currently investing in yourself to achieve the results you long for?

11. List three books/videos that you will read or watch in service of your goals. Set a deadline for reading or watching these resources.

    i. _____

    ii._____

    iii._____

KEEPING OUR COMMITMENTS: FINDING OUR SWAGGER

What are some of the feelings you have toward this change?
(Circle all that apply.)

Supportive Feelings

AFFECTIONATE	AMAZED	APPRECIATIVE	AMUSED
BRAVE	BLISSFUL	CALM	CONFIDENT
CONTENT	COMPASSIONATE	COMFORTABLE	CURIOUS
ENCOURAGED	EMPOWERED	EXCITED	EXUBERANT
FULFILLED	FREE	FORTUNATE	GRATEFUL
HAPPY	INVIGORATED	INVOLVED	IMPULSIVE
INTERESTED	INSPIRED	JOYFUL	LOVED
LIBERATED	LUCKY	MOVED	MELLOW
OPTIMISTIC	PEACEFUL	PLEASED	PROUD
PASSIONATE	RELAXED	RELIEVED	REFRESHED
RENEWED	RESTORED	REVIVED	SATISFIED
SURPRISED	SAFE	STIMULATED	SYMPATHETIC
THANKFUL	TRUSTED		

Unsupportive Feelings

ABANDONED	ALONE	ASHAMED	BRUSHED OFF
BEATEN DOWN	CONFUSED	CUT DOWN	CRITICIZED
DISAPPROVED	DISCOURAGED	DEHUMANIZED	DISRESPECTED
EXHAUSTED	EMBARRASSED	FEARFUL	HUNGRY
HUMILIATED	IGNORED	INSIGNIFICANT	INFERIOR
INSULTED	INVALIDATED	LABELED	LECTURED TO
LONELY	MISUNDERSTOOD	MOCKED	NEGLECTED
OFFENDED	PUT DOWN	REJECTED	RESENTFUL
RIDICULED	STEREOTYPED	STIFLED	TEASED
THREATENED	UNDERESTIMATED	UNHEARD	UNKNOWN
UNIMPORTANT	UNINFORMED	UNLOVED	UNSUPPORTED
UNWANTED	UNCARED FOR	UNAPPROVED	UNAWARE
UNABLE	WORTHLESS		

1. How much do you agree with the following statement: "I am completely responsible for my own life and circumstances, and through my choices, I create and co-create my reality"? Why?

2. Change doesn't understand impossible, but often, it seems like impossible is all we face. What obstacles stand between you and the results you desire?

3. When might those unsupportive feelings prevent you from keeping commitments, and how can you prepare in advance so that you can stand up under the negativity?

4. We fear what we don't understand, and we avoid what we fear As it relates to the change you face, what are you most afraid of?

5. What previous shortfalls do you need to forgive yourself for and how will moving beyond your history help your future?

6. In what areas do you get slippery or try to weasel away or hide out? How do you plan to handle that?

7. What measurements or personal metrics will you use to gauge your progress?

YOUR SET LIST

Start Date: _____

Cover Song: _____

Seven-Day Check in: _____

Two-Week Check in: _____

Thirty-Day Check in: _____

Transition Date:_____

Sampled Song: _____

Seven-Day Check in: _____

Two-Week Check in: _____

Thirty-Day Check in: _____

Transition Date:_____

Original Song: _____

Seven-Day Check in: _____

Two-Week Check in: _____

Thirty-Day Check in: _____

EPILOGUE

A MOMENT OF HONESTY

When we first decided to write this book, we were motivated by hopes of progressing our speaking careers. We envisioned presenting to large audiences and then selling our book in the back of the room, as we figured the book world and the music world are similar in a number of ways: getting your song on the charts is similar to hitting the "bestseller" list, and the quest to perform at a great venue exists in the speaker's world as well. So, we embarked on our journey and started writing this book almost two years ago.

After a year of writing, we had a powerfully emotional pile of crap. To use a music reference, it was a "mash-up" that just wasn't working—like George Strait and Eminem on the same track. Those are two great artists, no doubt, but without alignment as to the purpose of the collaboration, it was a hot mess.

We decided to reach out for some help. It wasn't until we partnered with our book architect, Justin Spizman, that things came together. He walked us through the Cover Song Approach to writing a book and helped us find our literary OOV. Our writing improved with each chapter, and we got fewer and fewer editing notes from Justin. As we researched the science behind change, we realized that the potential this book has to create significant impact in someone's life is incredible. Our focus shifted from "us" and our stories to "you" and yours. That's when the magic happened for us.

People like Molly Fletcher, Paul Redman, Rob Bell, Andrea Kremer, Jim Knight, Alan Schaefer, Duane Cummings, Kevin Lilly Jr, Andrew and Ryan Beltran, and the Sheehy family enthusiastically agreed to participate. A radio legend like Delilah not only said yes but did so while sitting in a limousine with her family on the way to being inducted into the Broadcasters Hall of Fame. Things like this don't happen by accident.

We would be remiss if we didn't share with you that our faith is central to our lives. For us, the process of initiating and surviving change is laden with dangerously unbearable burdens. Have you heard the common saying, "God doesn't give you more than you can handle"? We have all heard it, and many of us have given it the finger when the world is crashing in around us. The fact is, that saying is simply not true. That sentence is not true because it is missing a single incredibly important word: alone. "God doesn't give you more than you can handle alone."

We are built for community: community first with our creator and then with one another. We are designed to share and carry each other's burdens. Please don't see this as a heavy "religious" hand. That is most certainly not our intention. It is a simply a hand reaching out, telling you that we are here—no matter what you believe—willing and ready to walk with you through the changes in your life.

Jim would still weigh 430 pounds without the help of a loving and caring community. Theo would simply not be here at all. It was community that helped us stay on track, maintain our commitments, and hold on to hope as we faced what we couldn't face alone. The goal for Rock 'n' Roll with It is to gather together a community of people who either long for the type of change that will allow them to live the life they envisioned or who wish to overcome the unintentional change that has shaken the very foundation on which they stand.

In that light, we will be creating a community to share our successes and struggles. You can find that online community at rocknrollwithit. com, a social networking community. In addition, we will hit the road and travel around the country, doing experiential workshops where we will get our hands dirty together and stand arm in arm to help you create a set list that will produce your desired results.

Our journey in writing this book has been one of the most rewarding experiences of our lives. It has brought us closer together and lit a fire in our bellies to change what's possible for anyone willing to listen. From the bottom of our hearts, thank you for taking the time to read this. We pray you will be inspired to change what's possible for your life. If you aren't ready for that type of change, that is okay—for now. But refusing to embrace change is ignoring the elephant in the room.

In this case, the elephant is wearing a leather-studded hat, choker, vest, and chaps and is listening to Judas Priest on his iPod. If you think you can ignore that, then, "You've got another think comin'."

We figured ending with a Judas Priest metaphor is as rock 'n' roll as it gets.

Rock 'n' roll with it, friends.
Best,

Brant and Jim

POINT HOPE PARTNERSHIP

CHANGE HAS ALREADY BEGUN!

We have partnered with an incredible organization for the launch of this book. A portion of every sale will go to support the fantastic work of Point Hope.

Point Hope was founded by the international radio personality Delilah in 2005, who realized she could choose to take part in changing lives. While she might only be one person, she knew she could choose to be one person who makes a difference in the lives of children in need. The vision she imparted to Point Hope was to be a voice for forgotten children, a reality which has been happening in the United States and West Africa since then.

Point Hope's domestic mission focuses on bringing awareness and change to the plight and needs of children in the foster care system—and those aging out—in America. They host fun mentoring events for those same children (the "Teenista" for teen girls and the "Hoo-Rah" for teen boys) and provide "Totes of Hope 4 Teens" to children in foster care. A "tote" or duffle bag from Point Hope is filled with personal hygiene materials and everyday items, including some items of comfort. This is a simple gesture, but it provides humanity and hope.

At the same time, Point Hope sheds light on harsh truths for those who are unaware that many of the teens in foster care are at risk of becoming modern slaves and being kidnapped or enticed into human trafficking. Point Hope encourages people to be aware of the signs of human trafficking and to train themselves to see what is often happening right in front of them.

Point Hope realized they needed to expand their focus. Point Hope Ghana, also established in 2005, began effecting change in Liberian refugee camps within Ghana. 80 percent of children in Ghana suffer from some form of malnutrition, and 3.5 million people rely on unsafe water for survival, a situation which leaves many vulnerable to the spread of diseases and brings death to children and their families. Point Hope saw that there was no singular or universal solution to these problems, but rather, change is achieved by treating each child, family, and community as a unique case.

Point Hope's integrated, holistic model has twelve foundational pillars that work together to restore hope, find purpose, and save lives: Living Water (fresh, clean water); Nutrition; Agriculture; Nutrition Education; Early Childhood Education; Basic Education; Special Needs and Disabilities; Higher Education; Skills Training; Entrepreneurship; Health and Welfare; Point Hope Village (for widows and orphans to have homes where they have forever families).

The best news for people who want to help? A few dedicated individuals do all this work. In fact, Point Hope isn't a large organization, which makes change that much more possible and immediate. They have dedicated funding for administrative expenses, so every cent of donated funds goes directly to operations, programs, and projects where they are helping people help themselves through sustainable methods.

Point Hope is determined to be an agent of change, to be a voice and an advocate for forgotten children. We are imploring you to join with us! What can *one* person do? One person can change the life of at least one other person—and that can change the world!

To learn more, please go to www.pointhope.org, follow their Facebook pages (Point Hope and Point Hope Ghana), and find them on Twitter and Instagram at PointHopeOrg.

Point Hope is a 501(c)3, not for profit organization, based in Washington State, EIN 20-1216129.

ABOUT THE AUTHORS

BRANT MENSWAR

Brant Menswar is an award-winning musician, author, and sought after speaker. Through his work as Managing Partner with Banding People Together, he has helped clients navigate change and influenced the collaborative culture of companies like NASA, ESPN, Baxter Pharmaceuticals, Microsoft, Cisco, Honeywell, Sony Pictures, Hard Rock International, Hilton, Focus Brands, SunTrust and dozens of others. As the front man for the acclaimed blues/soul band, Big Kettle Drum, Menswar's voice has been described as "gritty and magnificent" by industry titans like Billboard and Sirius/XM Radio. Brant serves on the Board of Directors for the Children's Home Society of Florida. He is a graduate of Florida Southern College.

JIM TRICK

Jim Trick is a certified life coach, author, speaker and acclaimed folk musician. Trained by the prestigious Coach Training Institute and certified by the International Coach Federation, Jim has built a highly successful coaching practice in Marblehead, MA. Through his work with Banding People Together, Jim has helped organizations like Focus Brands, Hampton, SunTrust, NASA, ESPN and Cisco build a culture of effective collaboration. He is a regular guest lecturer at Berklee College of Music. Jim has founded two inner city food outreach programs for the homeless and continues to live his passion of working with people who want to personally and professionally live with greater freedom, fulfillment and success.